Chasing Maine's Second

Cover Art: "Two Kayaks," John Bozin,
Hebron Gallery, Monson, Maine

MICHAEL NORTON

Chasing Maine's Second

A FIGHT FOR CONGRESS IN PARADISE

Blue Pickerel LLC
Yarmouth, Maine

DEDICATION

For my parents, Cath and Vern Norton, discoverers of the North Woods.

He grooved on the place. She made sense of it and stopped the idea of winter "in a tin can" before it started.

Table of Contents

PART ONE

On the Ballot

CHASING MAINE'S SECOND

1

STANDING OUT

Cadillac Mountain is a cooperative geologic wonder. People drive to this round top. They find seats, or stand, on granite bulged here 420 million years ago, waiting for the show.

This October morning, like all October mornings, 200 or so people are hunkered in predawn darkness. Some joke about decisions to get out of beds or crawl from sleeping bags at nearby campsites.

A Cadillac Mountain sunrise in Maine's Acadia National Park is easier than other bucket list items. Still, nature gets a say. The surrounding ocean bats away moonlight, suspiciously warm, and pushes wind at the mountainside. At 1,500 feet above sea level, the guests are the first to feel and to see the sun rise on the United States.

The dark Schoodic Peninsula and smattered islands guide the eye to an eastern horizon with a nothing-more-to-see attitude. The view is nearly 360 degrees. When the sun rises above the distant rim, waiting gets erased; like you are waking from anesthesia. You are in darkness, dampness, thin air and wind. Then, you are bathed in hypernatural light, reflected color, ocean, sky, and distant clapboards. Hunkered people are now upright, looking at deep Atlantic blue and frisky skies in all directions. Some have cameras or easels out. They try to capture it. Good luck.

Cadillac Mountain is an eastern edge on an old American frontier. This fall, in 2018, there is a clamor for the place to help settle a fight for control of the U.S. Congress. More money is getting spent on politics here — by a factor of ten — than the routine just a few years back.

Among people who live here — spread out across places just as beautiful as Cadillac and rarely visited — things are quiet. This old place has produced more notable political leaders than most, in part because it is less hot-blooded about politics. The citizenry here are independent, older and worn, sometimes quirky. They are not boiling with anger; they also are not, as some might say on the docks, "happy as clams at high water."

The shorthand for the congressional district that dedicated operatives on both sides are battling to capture is "the Second" — meaning the second of two districts in Maine, a state of 1.3 million people. The First District owns Maine's largest city — Portland, to the south — and has an umbilical cord to the go-go economy of Massachusetts. The Second — north and above what some locals call "the Volvo line" at the Androscoggin River — has a bit of a chip on its shoulder.

Political operatives care about this place because it has proven capacity to vote for either a Democrat or a Republican. In 2008, Barack Obama was elected president by 12 percent here. He won re-election by 8 percent before Donald Trump carried the place with a 10-percent edge. Academics who take a longer view than operatives are curious about this last result. When a stubborn-to-change place like the Second takes a turn in politics it matters — a possible signal that rural places everywhere are realigning to a new politics and new appeals. More election data — from elections like this one in 2018 — are needed to know if the Second has more on its mind than the routines of readying for winter.

This fall's fixation for national Democratic and Republican Party operatives is whether the Second can be one of 23 congressional seats that Democrats need to take control of the U.S. House of Representatives. There are 435 House seats. Most are so locked down by party preference — in some cases gerrymandered to be that way — that only about two in 10 can be won by either side.

On a spreadsheet of about 60 or so districts that could go either way this fall, most are in the suburbs of states like Virginia, California, and Minnesota. The Second of Maine is a big-footed stranger on this list. So large that you could fit three New Jerseys and a Rhode Island in it and still have 320 square miles to spare.

Within all that rugged space, there is not much resembling what political strategists would call a suburb. There are a handful of small cities, many towns, townships, and even things called "unorganized territories." You can drive to Boston from the southernmost point of the Second in two and a half hours. Still, in this the largest congressional district east of the Mississippi, you find no gaggle of minivans.

The novelty of the place is not sparing the Second from standard election treatment — both political parties are fire-hosing voters here with digital and broadcast campaign ads. Combined, the two campaigns, and their supporting political action committees (PACs), are spending $31 million, mainly on television ads. This in a place where TV ads are cheap and where, only a few years back, $1 million dollars was plenty of cash to run any campaign.

Stranger still, those dollars are chasing "swing" voters who barely even care to play. Daniel Bailey, the 30ish owner of Zimmie's Comics in Lewiston, has customers who get all ginned up about politics; not him; he may not vote. "I'm not into politics," Bailey says. "Too much arguing."

The vastness of the district — stretching from a long, mountainous border with New Hampshire, rimming around a 611-mile international border with Canada to an ocean coast with more shore than Maryland, Delaware and Rhode Island combined — makes the Second a frontier apart from its sources of capital investment in the rest of tradition-bound New England. The place lives extremes. Ambitious people have come and gone for centuries here. They try big things, leaving benefits, pain, and puzzles.

In a venture just before the Great Depression, and in the shadow of Cadillac Mountain near Bar Harbor, auto industrialists supported a college professor focused on the health research value of mice. Decades later, the Jackson Laboratory is a global genetics research hub for 7,000 strains of genetically defined mice used in research worldwide. Jackson itself has researchers in Maine, Connecticut, and California focused on the genetic and molecular courses of disease. Cancer, Alzheimer's, and potential for individualized genetic treatment are what they are working on down from the mountain.

Farther north, in Aroostook County, the U.S. government deployed enough B-52 bombers in the 1950s with nuclear weapons to create a real — or as military strategists would say "credible" — threat of obliteration for the Soviet Union. Planes can reach the European half of Russia more directly by flying over the Arctic Circle from here. This made the empty miles of flat ground in the far north — already cleared for potato fields — attractive to U.S. Air Force Gen. Curtis LeMay. Loring Air Force Base near the town of Limestone closed in 1994. A relic of the Cold War, Loring's mission got replaced by missiles and submarines elsewhere.

A hiker in the central Maine mountains can look down on fall colors radiating off Flagstaff Lake and miss a harsher detail. Thirty feet under that lake is a town called Flagstaff. Residents cleared out in 1950 to make way for a dam that flooded their town and enabled hydropower generation downstream.

The noisy 2018 election season is not venturing deeply into the details of the Second's economic or social history. Most voters do not know that the plummeting paper-manufacturing employment they see today is a version of a story the Second had seen many times; more times, in fact, than just about any other American place. The details do not matter. Political strategists mash it up for motivation anyway — blaming global trade for something caused by technology or technology for something caused by trade, when it suits.

There is shorthand for all of it. Newspapers in southern Maine call the Second "hardscrabble." The Boston Globe previews the congressional race with a description of the district as "filled with forests, lobsters, and blueberries." The simple story — a postcard and pain, all-in-one — is comfortable for outsiders and national campaigns.

2

THE BIG MACHINE

The contest for the Second matches a tenacious congressman against a Democrat seeking to be the first from his party ever to unseat an incumbent Republican in this rugged collection of counties.

U.S. Rep. Bruce Poliquin is 65. His challenger is close to half his age. Both men know politics. Neither is a natural. Both understand that in the fall of 2018 the journey to win any congressional seat is national; most urgently, a hunt for national dollars. The two candidates, and PACs supporting them, are raising and using that $31 million — blasting old records with ten times more campaign spending than the routine here just ten years ago. Partisan desires — stymying President Trump versus holding influence on taxes, regulation, and federal judge appointments — keep the money train rolling to this far northern corner of the republic.

Just 38 percent of the people giving to the two candidates live in Maine. This plummets below 20 percent when limited to donors who have an address in the Second District. Federal Election Commission spending reports show an identical anatomy for the flow of those dollars in both campaigns. You find the brain in Washington, D.C., directing the lifeblood: television ads.

The $4.6 million raised by the Democrat through the middle of October goes largely to Maine television outlets and consultants based in Washington or traveling frequently to Washington. Similarly, Congressman Poliquin's $3.9 million goes to television and a right-hand consultant, Brent Littlefield, based in Washington.

Outside groups — also shoveling cash into this small media market — add another $23.9 million to the pot. Democratic supporters have the edge there too, outpacing Poliquin $14.1 million to $9.8 million. Saturation takes away much of the value of owning this spending edge. A million-dollar ad buy can dominate Maine media for many weeks.

The Democrat, known only to party loyalists, needs all that campaign cash more urgently. His team understands that challengers lose congressional races all the time on what amounts to a technicality — they just do not have the marketing dollars to get their name on par with the politician who already has the gig. Incumbents won 97 percent of congressional races in 2016 — close to the historic norm in this long-shot derby for challengers.

Challengers need to introduce themselves in a market game that is akin to selling laundry detergent against Tide. Your liquid goo might be good, but everyone knows Tide. Political marketing is more zero-sum than laundry detergent too. You cannot just shave off some loyal customers and make a living in electoral politics. You need half the people to know you exist and to choose you. On the bright side, there are fewer choices; and if you win, you are the new Tide.

There are fascinating political races across the nation this fall — a close U.S. Senate race in Texas; a governor's race in Georgia confronting voting rights questions that a place like the Second can barely imagine. No one notices that the ancient Second of Maine is eclipsing heat elsewhere in unexpected ways, revealing a subtly better yardstick to measure whether the United States is going to live up to its creed or decompensate.

Experiments happen in the Second, always have. Voter choices are set to get tallied differently here, in an election experiment and reform that could spread to states and alter the calculus of all U.S. politics. There are other telling quirks too. Unnoticed local races in the rural Second offer strong clues about the causes and trajectory of Trumpism. One small town is voting on whether to euthanize itself. In another rural pocket, a young man is so alarmed by Trump's election that he moves home from Asia to run for the state Legislature. Maine's nationalized throw-down for a congressional seat seeks attention and pulls in dollars. What it means to be a lost frontier, beautiful and not quite fitting in the bigger machine, is down the ballot and out in the woods.

3

RANKED CHOICE VOTING

The first thing you notice in Jim Melcher's office is the plastic action figure of former Minnesota governor and professional wrestler Jesse Ventura.

Within minutes, Melcher is channeling the voluble Ventura.

"Internationally, people care about RCV!" Melcher exclaims. "This is the first U.S. state to use RCV in a statewide election, period! The first state to use it in a federal election, period!"

Melcher, a political scientist in the Second's western mountain town of Farmington, tosses around jargon like "RCV" for the same reason he cherishes his Ventura action figure. The guy is passionate about politics — its process, candidates, ups, downs, in-betweens, and rules of operating.

This fall, an election innovation is rolling out in Melcher's backyard, prompting calls to his office at the University of Maine at Farmington from European journalists and inquiries from his U.S. political science colleagues. Behind these wonky interactions is another reason to watch the Second in the age of Trump.

Ranked choice voting, RCV in Melcher's lingo, is sometimes called instant runoff. Used in Australia, it is especially effective at enabling third-party or independent candidates to run and be more than just spoilers. Voters get a ballot that invites them to rank their candidate choices when there are more than two in the race. Their ranked choices — second, third, and so on choices, depending on the size of the field — are considered only if no candidate gets a majority. Voters also can pass on the option of making any additional choices and vote only for their favorite. The concept is like the handful of U.S. states that have runoff elections when the top-two vote-getters do not get an election-night majority. Runoffs between top-two candidates happen a month or so later in those states. With ranked choice, there is no new campaign. The ballot records any candidate rankings a voter wants to make. When the voter's first choice is mathematically eliminated from having a shot at a majority, their lesser preferences can roll up to nudge a top candidate to a winning majority.

This is insider stuff, not what most voters in the Second or elsewhere are talking about. Still, as Melcher knows, influential people with serious financial backing would like to see ranked choice succeed in Maine and jump to other states.

FairVote, a nonprofit and leading proponent of ranked choice, spends more than $3 million annually promoting election reforms. The eclectic board of FairVote includes Krist Novoselic, former bandmate of the late Kurt Cobain in Nirvana, along with academic experts and operatives ranging from libertarian to the left. Maine is the most important beachhead for ranked choice in the United States so far. Backers seeking to shield their electoral reform from today's hyperpartisanship pivot away from the reason ranked choice got a chance here: Maine adopted ranked choice voting because Maine experienced a Donald Trump-style politician winning a Donald Trump-style election before the United States knew what that looked like. Paul LePage, the citizen mayor of Waterville's 20,000 residents and general manager of a salvage retailer, won a seven-candidate Republican primary for governor in 2010 with 37 percent of the vote. LePage flew below the radar of his Republican primary opponents. The other six candidates had better conventional connections. One had close ties to both U.S. Senators Olympia Snowe and Susan Collins. All that mattered not-at-all in the split-up, seven-candidate field. LePage was unique: A one-man tea party of New England grievance and penny-pinching, available to anyone who wanted to rattle experts. LePage's general election competition included two viable independent candidates and a Democrat. LePage won with 38 percent of the vote. With the same suddenness that America woke to Donald Trump in 2016, sensible Maine woke to a new variety of governor in 2010.

As governor, LePage mused about drug dealers with names like "Shifty" coming to Maine from outside the state and "half the time impregnating a young, white girl." He cited "hepatitis C, tuberculosis, AIDS, HIV, the 'Ziki' (meaning Zika virus) fly" as hazards brought by political asylum seekers. His cadence of half-baked or mean — never much of a staple in Maine politics before — rarely paused. When Democrats whiffed in another multicandidate field in 2014, LePage got re-elected with 48 percent.

As LePage said, "I was Donald Trump before Donald Trump." The solid plurality that had always been "never LePage," and failed twice in gubernatorial elections to oust him, became the base for two statewide referendums supporting ranked choice voting. They won both times with 52 percent. Nine of the 10 counties in the Second — including the two largest counties — voted against ranked choice voting. The majorities putting the new method into election law statewide came from southern Maine. Ranked choice supporters had hoped their reform could be nonpartisan. Instead, Maine voters found their tribes on the matter.

The best hope for national reformers is that the implementation goes smoothly. Ranked choice is mainly a technical reform. In academic modeling of past election returns, ranked choice is rarely a game-changer. Ninety-five percent of the time it just affirms the win of the candidate who won a plurality on election night. This October in Maine, the Second is signaling that it might not play by that math. There are two independent candidates in the race, both earnest people without a snowball's chance in the Bahamas of getting more than a few percentage points. The most credible poll shows the two major party candidates for Congress tied at 45 percent each.

4

A TOWN SURRENDERS

The main election event in the Second is running conventionally. Congressman Poliquin threads a needle, never saying whether he voted for President Trump and painting a picture of Democratic central planning on matters like guns should he not be returned to Congress.

The Democrat is disciplined, threading a different needle. He eschews the love flowing to more progressive Democrats in other states and pounds away with poll-tested messages around health-care security and regular-Joe commitment to working Mainers.

None of this is unimportant, and none of it captures the depth of hurt in the Second. The place has been withering economically for 150 years. The most recent acceleration in that process took hold 20 years ago when the digital age put a fresh pounding on paper manufacturing. Without public spending on health care and education, even some larger communities in the Second are fragile enough to disappear.

Elections down the ballot can tell you things about decay, hope, and despair in the Second that the congressional candidates just do not reach. One election like this is happening in the tiny town of Atkinson. No one outside of the 300 people in Atkinson is watching this race. The ballot proposal — requiring a two-thirds vote of residents — is to vote Atkinson out of existence.

Drive through Atkinson on any October day and you see a rural place where a rational person would choose to live. The broad Piscataquis River, the town's northern border, and Alder Stream at its center, are colorful and welcoming. The place hardly qualifies as the remotest of outposts. The regional center town of Dover-Foxcroft, with 4,000 people, a hospital, and a public high school that doubles as a private academy, is just seven miles away. Some people commute to the city of Bangor, thirty-four miles away.

The fury for many in Atkinson is that they cannot afford to stay a town. They point the finger at government and outsiders.

"The fault lies with a government that turns a stone ear to the plight of its rural towns," Andy Torbett, Atkinson resident and polemicist for de-organizing the town, says. "Out-of-state groups and land barons cannot be given a free hand to destroy the economies of small-town Maine, while at the same time operating at the expense of those same towns."

This story is complicated. The idea that outsiders destroyed the place has holes. The farm and forestry businesses of Atkinson have been fragile for more than 100 years. The town's population peaked at 897 in 1860. Still, there is something essential to hear from Atkinson.

The issue driving Atkinson's attempt at municipal hari-kari is taxes. Their property-tax base is eroding — an erosion made faster and complete by a state regulatory element that pits traditional users of the land against land conservationists in a stubborn divide.

The rub is a long-standing tax law called Tree Growth. It allows any parcel of twelve or more acres to be managed for growing trees and taxed for that purpose only. This avoids being taxed at a higher value for all potential uses, such as putting up a summer camp near a lake or Alder Stream.

Tree Growth was established to make it more viable for large growers to stay in the game of growing big tracts and to keep important industries, like sawmills and paper mills, viable. The law had the added benefit of helping small-woodlot owners who risked seeing their family land climb in value, forcing them — because of higher tax bills — to sell out. If they joined in the requirement of Tree Growth, these owners — just like the big industrial players — paid only for the use they intended. That commitment lowered their tax valuation and their property taxes.

The landowner commitment to Tree Growth is firm. If any owner wants to get out of that commitment, they must pay the higher rate of property tax for all the years they were in Tree Growth, plus a penalty. Lawmakers did not fully envision when the state Legislature passed Tree Growth in 1972 that the law could be a method for anyone who wanted to conserve land at lower cost to do so.

There are other provisions in state law that allow for preservation of land without paying full taxable value, including easements and open space options. Still, the fact that Tree Growth was getting used as a tool for owners with the intention of preserving land long-term in its natural state forever irritated traditionalists.

In Atkinson, that played out on the map. Roughly two-thirds of the town is owned by a preservation group out of Vermont and a land conservationist who lives in Dover-Foxcroft and made his fortune in New York City real estate. All that land is in Tree Growth or similar legal provisions, making it impossible for the town to tax the land at a higher value. The mil rate per $1,000 of value in Atkinson climbed above $23 for houses and farms in town that were not in Tree Growth.

The emotional smack in the jaw for people who live or farm in the town – many for generations and who do not want the forever commitment of Tree Growth or do not have enough acres to qualify — is not deniable. Outsiders without a stake in Atkinson, intentionally or not, are making it harder for the place to stay a town. The town has no path forward to grow its tax base — more than two-thirds of the place already is locked down in provisions that do not allow development. Torbett and others see the vote as limiting the damage from unsustainable property tax rates for those stuck in the full-pay bucket.

If approved, the change will dramatically lower the tax rate for everyone in town, down from $23 to $6 per $1,000 of real estate value. The change will sever the relationship with the school district. Ironically, it also will let outsiders — the county and the state — decide which roads are kept. Management of the school relationship and transportation for about 20 school children in town will be handled at the state level. Backers of the vote, fiercely in favor of local control, must cede their control and de-organize their town to get a lower, more sustainable tax bill. This is what it means to be rural in places like the Second. Sometimes your town goes away, and no one notices or cares much about the details of how it happened.

5

A SON COMES HOME

Tyler Adkins grew up twenty-four miles northwest of Atkinson, in the slate-quarry town of Monson. It was still a stable place with 750 people when Tyler pedaled around Pleasant Street in the 1990s. His dad was a logger; his mom was a hairdresser. "My favorite smells growing up were diesel fuel and perms," he says.

Adkins is typical of what the towns in every corner of the Second have produced for 170 years now — young people prepared in public schools and communities who leave to do big things far away.

He liked growing up in Monson. The now 34-year-old says it was simply understood when he went off to St. Michael's College in Vermont that he would make his life elsewhere. "I was one of those."

Humble teachers were his role models, motivating his first adult decision to study history and become a teacher. Adkins gets riled to this day when he talks about his first faculty advisor at college — "this guy who thought he was so special," he says, but who had no interest in him or any student. Adkins tweaked his major to political science to evade the self-important prof and find an invested educator. The move reflected a trait of rural Maine people — not always verbal in their self-advocacy, and yet, always profoundly pissed off when someone does not hear them or do their job.

Studying abroad in Copenhagen during his years at St. Michael's opened Adkins' eyes to another reality about himself and the Ivy League tribe he was now hanging with in Europe. "It was like, 'Oh, you are just as stupid as the rest of us,'" he says. "There's nothing different here."

He earned a graduate school scholarship at Lund University in Sweden. The program brought 40 students from around the globe together to focus on environmental studies and sustainability science. This deepened Adkins' interest in distributed energy systems — wind or solar power generation on a small scale at specific commercial or residential sites. In New York City after graduation, Adkins landed a job with UGE International, a distributed energy start-up. There were bounce-backs to home in Piscataquis County during his college years, and each time Adkins scrambled to get back to places where his new friends were — places like New York and San Francisco, places that would have opportunities like the one he found with UGE.

At first, Adkins says, some projects he worked on for UGE were demonstrations, not ready to go it alone without subsidy from the customer. Then, the solar market changed. The Chinese got in the game of making solar panels. This dropped the per-watt cost of projects by 80 percent. Adkins had spent two years developing distributed systems in the Philippines for UGE as a regional director. Solar — once constrained to markets where electricity costs were high enough to justify the cost of installation, like the Philippines — was trending to a more favorable cost structure. Business was good on his side of the world and looking better everywhere.

Still in the Philippines late in 2016, Adkins was due to transfer back to New York soon to continue running the now-mature Philippines business remotely and work on other projects. He recalls taking in the U.S. presidential election. He had written off "the political operative thing as not for me" eight years earlier after helping the Democratic Party in Piscataquis County. On Nov. 8, he expected comfortable news viewing, with a 12-hour time difference providing a late-morning view of the inevitable President Hillary Clinton. Instead, Adkins got rocked by a novel picture from the states — Donald Trump winning the presidency. The Maine man's life experience with the cause of Trump's election spiked his frustration at the sight. He knew that places like Monson were delivering for Trump. He believed they were better than Trump. He believed they were getting conned.

The next morning, Adkins made a leap. "I got up and I said, 'You are going to go home and you are going to run for office. That's what you have to do,'" he recalls.

Adkins renegotiated the terms of his return to the United States with his company. He works remotely now from Monson, between his company's North American locations in New York and Toronto, relying on email and travel. He is running this fall for the state Legislature as an independent, seeking to represent Monson, ten other towns, and unorganized territory in the region.

Some voters, he says, think he is the young Democrat running for Congress when he knocks on their door. They are about the same age. Most days, Adkins leaves the campaign trail thinking he has a shot. His energy — and showing up at the door in places where no candidates go —earn respect. Lynwood "Guy" Turner, a select board member in the 150-person town of Willimantic, credits Adkins for visiting his kitchen table.

"We had a nice chat," Turner says. "I talked to him about local decision-making."

Adkins keeps his focus on three needs he sees holding the region back — expanded broadband access, lower health-care costs, and more workforce training. "The response I am getting is overwhelmingly positive," he says.

It is not possible to stack the odds against the young man from Monson any higher. His opponent, incumbent Republican state Rep. Paul Stearns, had no challengers in his prior two elections. He won with about 82 percent both times. Yes, a plurality of voters did leave their ballots blank, but Stearns is not a guy who enrages anyone. He is known more as neighbor than party politician. He retired as the school superintendent and lives in Guilford, the largest of the small towns he and Adkins are competing in.

Ironically, given Adkins' green-energy resume, the former expat also is contending with a little-known Green Party candidate. The Second is quirky that way — two uncontested election cycles and now Adkins and a Green have come out of the woodwork. Adkins gets no shot at any votes siphoned to the

Green Party candidate. Ranked choice voting applies only to statewide primaries and federal elections.

Adkins does not care. He and his younger brother John are knocking on 3,000 doors spread across 500 square miles. They believe their neighbors are rutted in a hopeless future without basics like broadband coverage. They will try to explain it. Their hope is that youth and energy can budge the status quo.

PART TWO

Old Ground

6

THOREAU

"There stands the city of Bangor, fifty miles up the Penobscot, at the head of navigation for vessels of the largest class, the principal lumber depot on this continent, with a population of twelve thousand, like a star on the edge of night, still hewing at the forests of which it is built, already overflowing with the luxuries and refinement of Europe, and sending its vessels to Spain, to England, and to the West Indies for its groceries — and yet only a few axe-men have gone "up river" into the howling wilderness which feeds it."
Henry David Thoreau, The Maine Woods

There is no way to understand the playing field for hopefuls like Adkins — or the national gladiators fighting for the congressional seat — without looking back.

The Second is an old place, worthy of watching because it has lived, many times, the ambiguities of commerce and politics that breathless cable news talkers and conniving D.C. operatives believe are new.

There are characters, some from the Second and some from away, who put light on how the Second arrived at the crossroads of its 2018 ballot.

The first is Henry David Thoreau, writer, observer, and early person from away — or flatlander, as the locals now call these types. Thoreau hiked and paddled Maine's North Woods three times, in 1846, 1853, and 1857. His account, published in 1862 after his death, is a naturalist's travelogue of vast forests and rivers east of Monson and the 119-square-mile Moosehead Lake.

The Maine Woods — nearly invisible when it was published — went on to reach millions in the 20th century, becoming international sheet music for naturalists. Thoreau inspired a religiosity about wild places when he wrote about the Second's mountains, rivers, and lakes, and about his experience living in nature in Walden, published in 1854. The founders of many U.S. national parks trace their visions to reading Thoreau.

Maine lumbermen and Native Americans of the Penobscot guide Thoreau. Early on, his party of travelers is put up near the East Branch of the Penobscot River at the camp of a man named McCauslin. Thoreau describes McCauslin as "a waterman twenty-two years now . . . settled here to raise supplies for the lumberers and himself." He praises that his host declines payment for his "true Scotch hospitality." Thoreau admits surprise, too, that the deeper he travels into the woods, the "more intelligent" and sophisticated he finds the locals. Pioneers like McCauslin are "men of the world," Thoreau says, contrasting them with the New Englanders back home in Concord, Massachusetts.

"If I were to look for a narrow, uninformed, and countrified mind," Thoreau writes during his 1846 trip, it would "not be in the backwoods of Maine."

The praise is equal parts tribute to North Woods character and score-settling with Thoreau's neighbors back on "the high road in Concord." Still, if Thoreau had it right, the communities in the rim counties of the Second today might be in line for that same dig. They are "settled" today and, in many ways, have a mindset modeled on Yankee places like Concord.

Along Thoreau's route there are more examples of what is seen in the North Woods today — in particular, local people engaging with the world in ways that outsiders do not always expect or understand. At one point, Thoreau is pleased to find a copy of Ralph Waldo Emerson's address on West Indian emancipation at a logging camp. He is told that the tract made two converts to the Liberty Party, an abolitionist party and one forerunner of the Republican Party.

His main character is the Maine landscape.

"The lakes are something which you are unprepared for: they lie up so high exposed to the light, and the forest is diminished to a fine fringe on their edges, with here and there a blue mountain, like amethyst jewels set around some jewel of the first water — so anterior, so superior to all the changes that are to take place on their shores, even now civil and refined, and fair, as they can ever be."

There would come a time when the politics around conserving or harvesting this land would heat to a constant temperature — with most locals and influential outsiders clearly staked to one side or the other. In the years of Thoreau's travels — the late 1840s and early 1850s — taming wilderness is accepted practice. Even in the most remote areas of old-growth forest, Thoreau would see tree stumps cut well above his head. These were Eastern pines sawed down in winter when the snowpack elevated the loggers. Winter buried any underbrush, making it possible to drag the downed trees over snow to river valleys with oxen or horses. The spring melt then speeded gigatons of trees to places like Orono, Belfast, and Bangor.

Thoreau toured during a forgotten flurry of development — decades that set up the first and, by far, most consequential economic transition of many lying ahead for counties in the Second.

7

POPE AND TALBOT

"Entered the harbor of San Francisco this day at one o'clock p.m. …We went ashore between 3 and 4 o'clock and found Balch (sea captain Lafayette Balch from Maine's northern coast), who had a house taken and we went to his place for the night, our house is situated on the side of a hill overlooking the harbor and when the moon came up it presented the most beautiful sight in the world, hundreds of ships lying all in sight with their lights and then the lights of the city as it is spread out before us presents a grand spectacle."

Frederic Talbot of East Machias, Maine,
diary, Dec. 1, 1849

There were many ambitious men downstream from Thoreau's woods in the 1840s. Two who represent the cycle of commercial advance and setback that became the Second's destiny are Andrew Jackson Pope and Frederic Talbot.

Both were scions of the Pope and Talbot family lumber operations in Washington County — the eastern-most place in the United States and a beehive then. In those years, national and international commerce got powered through Maine in ways unimaginable to anyone living in any part of the state today.

In the 1850s, Maine produced one-third of all the ship tonnage manufactured in the United States. Clipper ships, barks, brigs, and schooners were the engines of global and national trade then. Among 31 states, only New York and Pennsylvania produced more lumber than Maine. Coastal Washington County had 131 sawmills. Inland and closer to ocean-sized plots of trees, Bangor moved ships and lumber down the broad Penobscot River. Penobscot County had 195 sawmills.

The era is comparable to a tech boom. Rivers became supply chains that sprouted natural commercial hubs in their basins. Cities like Belfast, a terminus of the Penobscot River, became perfect spots to build. Lumber, including huge trees for ship masts and endless board feet for parts, flowed to the shipyards. In the two decades leading to a peak around 1850, the workers who crafted and outfitted those ships diversified their skills. The ancient Maine reputation for quality and hard work moored here.

As with tech, things changed. Extended members of the Pope and Talbot families were in various lumber and shipping businesses. Andrew and Frederic are important because they made a trip in 1849 from East Machias, Maine to San Francisco, crossing the Panama isthmus pre-canal with horses and canoes. Their voyage involved multiple steam ships, a foreshadowing of steel and steam replacing the elaborate engineering of sail.

When the fever for gold and other resources in California took hold, prominent Maine operators like Pope and Talbot trained their ambition on that new frontier. Just about every tree in Washington County had been cut by the late 1840s. The West was next. The West had a rush of people who needed lumber for buildings and ships. The West had more trees.

The Mainers were well positioned to take advantage. They had ships. They had the ship captains from places like East Machias on the coastal edge of Washington County. The daring part was getting their lumbering and sawmill equipment to places like California and what would become Washington state and Oregon. It required rounding Cape Horn at the tip of South America — a place known for unpredictable winds and icebergs that abolished ships with efficiency.

The men who pulled off these feats came to own a reputation in San Francisco and the Pacific Northwest, where they were called State of Mainers. Others chased gold. The Mainers chased trees, shipping contracts, finished lumber, and profits — all of which would sink new roots in the West Coast.

The employees of what would become the Pope and Talbot Paper Company in Port Gamble, Washington, made voyages many times through the 19th and 20th centuries from the Maine coast to the Pacific Northwest. They brought lumbering equipment and skilled shipping men from Maine to the west. In the 1940s, historian Stewart Holbrook noted conversations about this westward emigration of talent.

"I talked with many other older people in East Machias. Without exception they were sad that Pope & Talbot had constantly taken away their young folk for seventy years past; but they did not resent it. If it hadn't been Pope & Talbot, I was told, then it would have been somebody or something else."

It was true. There were waves of other changes coming from 1850 forward that would advance and then set back the coastal and inland counties of the Second. Steel and steam became the power in shipping, converting wooden boatbuilding over decades into a smaller, niche industry — high in quality, low in head count.

Like many of the lumber operators, farmers were leaving for the West — especially to the Midwest states of Iowa, Illinois, Minnesota, and Wisconsin. The land was richer for farming, not played out like an increasing amount in New England, and more plentiful. Railroads were transforming food into a more efficient, regional business. Farms that could specialize in certain crops had the edge. The so-called Yankee Exodus took hold across New England states. By the 1890s, between 10 and 15 percent of all farms in three large, inland counties of the Second — Oxford, Franklin, and Piscataquis — were abandoned. Most consider farm loss as a Depression-era, dust-bowl phenomenon. The Second got there first.

8

CHAMBERLAIN

"When we think of the tragedy of Little Round Top and look
for reasons or explanations which justify the suffering and
the death, it is no wonder we feel the need for legends."
Historian Thomas A. Desjardin, Lewiston, Maine

The people who put down those early roots in the Second were not bystanders.
They were aggressive in commerce, like Pope and Talbot. They were
experimenters in religion, like the Free Will Baptists.

Just about every varietal of ambition here hewed to the American
experiment too. The notion of a classic Greek republic fitted with American
nationalism and democratic values was hot stuff on this spread-out landscape.
Founders chose town names in the Second to tell you what they were thinking
— Greek virtues, Freedom and Unity, and founding heroes, Washington,
Jefferson, and Monroe, all sprouted on the map.

In the Civil War's test to the experiment, the Second engaged beyond its
modest population size, and lost a fresh share of its potential at places like
Fredericksburg, Virginia, shattering hearts at home with a completeness that
sending a son and daughter to new frontiers in Iowa or California could not
match.

Joshua Lawrence Chamberlain became the symbol of this era. He was born
in 1828 in Brewer. Across the Penobscot River from Bangor, Brewer was a
shipbuilding and brick-making companion in the busy Penobscot Bay.
Biographies of Chamberlain say his mother wanted him to be a preacher; his
father favored soldier. He took neither path. When the Civil War broke out,
Chamberlain was a professor of modern languages at Bowdoin College in
Brunswick, Maine. He came from a social station that could choose military
service or staying out of the war. He advocated that his students join the Union

cause and joined the 20th Maine Regiment himself as a lieutenant colonel more than one year into the fight.

"I fear, this war, so costly of blood and treasure, will not cease until men of the North are willing to leave good positions, and sacrifice the dearest personal interests, to rescue our country from desolation, and defend the national existence against treachery," he wrote of his reasoning to Maine's governor at the time.

Actor Jeff Daniels plays Chamberlain now in popular films about the Civil War. This is because the professor did something bold and desperate that some historians consider pivotal to the Union winning a battle and winning the war.

Chamberlain was leading his 20th Maine on the far-left end of the Union Army line during the second day of the Gettysburg battle. Out of ammunition and expecting to be run over by a larger Confederate force, Chamberlain ordered a bayonet charge from the regiment's position, a place called Little Round Top, downhill at the enemy. Stunned and exhausted, the Confederates surrendered. For preventing a possible turn in the Union line, many credit Chamberlain's regiment with saving the opportunity for the Union Army to win at Gettysburg the next day, making ultimate success inevitable for Lincoln's Union.

The most thorough historian of the event, Lewiston, Maine, native and historian Thomas Desjardin, grappled with dozens of accounts about what happened on that rocky hill. His conclusions: the 20th Maine was heroic on more days than just one and versions that celebrated Chamberlain for a textbook military maneuver were gliding past the adrenaline of war.

"While many imagine the legendary right wheel of the 20th Maine's left wing, the men who are said to have carried it out remembered something far more confused, with men running in every direction but the rear," Desjardin clarified.

Chamberlain is a storied symbol in all parts of Maine — a museum and statue honoring him stand in Brunswick, along with a statue in his hometown of Brewer. He is the hero story everyone wants to tell. More telling for the future of the frontier towns in the Second were the war casualties and the timing of those losses.

Maine lost more than 9,300 soldiers and sailors — men and women who posed as men to join — in the Civil War. Relative to population size, this was among the two or three states on the Union side with the most lives lost.

The war's timing deepened a stunting of the Second. The dynamic of community leaders moving west for more ambitious lumbering, shipping, and farming operations was in play before the war. Now, specific industries were taking setbacks. Cod and mackerel fishing were losing to Gloucester, Massachusetts, which was closer to urban markets and rail lines. War dead accelerated lost potential.

None of this spelled the end for rural Maine. There were natural resources to pair with industrial development still ahead. The counties of the Second adapted. New manufacturing — in lumber, textiles, leather — had some strength heading into the next century. Pulp and papermaking would emerge as the biggest employer of all and have a run that still has life.

Still, a pattern got set in the decades after the Civil War. The Second always changed to what was next. What was next was always more efficient and often not complementary to building a diverse, local economy. Against this backdrop, the counties of the Second kept developing their young people and, with regularity, exporting them to other places — places seen as forward-looking while the Second got tagged as backward.

9

MUSKIE

"We got to get Muskie, you know, out on a limb on some of these critical issues."

President Richard Nixon,
a 1972 recording in the Oval Office

Sixty-four years ago, Maine politics took a tectonic turn that no one saw coming.

Republicans — then the party of Lincoln — owned Maine politics from the Civil War to the 1950s.

Hero Joshua Lawrence Chamberlain was elected governor as a Republican four times. James G. Blaine, a newspaper editor who immigrated to his wife's native Maine, became speaker of the U.S. House of Representatives and a titan in Republican politics after the war. Blaine ran for president in 1884, losing narrowly to Grover Cleveland.

Even pushing out to 1954, there were few signs this dominance would change. In the five prior races for president, the Democratic nominee lost in Maine; Presidents Franklin Roosevelt and Harry Truman accounted for four of those failures.

The presidency was not on the ballot in 1954. Maine governor was, and late in the campaign calendar a young lawyer decided to get into that race on the Democratic side. His intent was to give Democrats a credible candidate in every statewide race and build plausibility for the future. There were 262,344 registered Republicans and only 99,389 Democrats in Maine then. Winning just was not the point.

The young lawyer was the son of an immigrant from Russian-occupied Poland. His father, Stephen Marciszewski, came to the United States in 1903. The father changed the family name to Muskie in 1914, a year when fear of foreigners bounced with a world war getting underway. The son grew up in the western mountains of the Second, in the mill town of Rumford, where his father opened a tailor shop. Young Muskie thought the first name his parents gave him — Edmund — was a little much. He liked Ed better.

Election night 1954 affirmed Republican dominance in the big jobs. Republicans won the U.S. Senate seat by 42,000 votes. They swept the then-three congressional seats. Standing apart was Ed Muskie. The Democrat, known mainly for wearing bow ties then, beat Republican Gov. Burton Cross by 22,000 votes. It is still a head-scratcher.

Muskie went on to have one of the most productive policy-making careers in 20th century American politics, as governor, U.S. senator, candidate for vice-president and president, and U.S. secretary of state. The Second's congressional race in 2018 is a contest between Republicans and Democrats because of Muskie's plodding, party-building work.

The Muskie career is revealing in other ways too. Once he became a senator, his accomplishments accrued more value to the nation than to home turf. He was a pure talent export from the Second, representative of the district's century-long assignment. Muskie pushed himself into topics like water quality that were dull, inside-stuff when he started in the Senate in 1959 and that later came to define the environmentalism we know today — a struggle between traditionalists who want a free hand for business and regulators who see health and environmental risks demanding government intervention.

Muskie guided the first federal clean air and clean water laws through the U.S. Senate. President Richard Nixon feared Muskie's pragmatist reputation and voter appeal, earning the Maine senator some dirty tricks that contributed to the faltering of his 1972 presidential primary bid.

Muskie got heat, too, from potential friends who — having gained clout with the public around the science and sight of environmental damage — were not sure the Senate's mode of compromise worked for them.

10

NADER

"Perhaps the single most effective antagonist of American business is Ralph Nader, who — thanks largely to the media — has become a legend in his own time and an idol of millions of Americans."

Lewis F. Powell, Jr.,
future U.S. Supreme Court Justice, 1971

Ralph Nader was still best-known for his indictment of auto safety, Unsafe at Any Speed, when he came to the topic of the Maine woods economy in 1973.

In an era of reform and activism, Nader could gather speed, fury, and a legal framework for continued attack better than more technically minded advocates. His environmentalism emerged, side by side with the careers of institutional leaders like Muskie, to bludgeon earlier, frontier assumptions about conquering wilderness. The mindset Nader blistered was so ingrained in the culture that even Thoreau mourned living trees during his treks in the Maine woods. He conceded their inevitable harvest to feed boomtowns like Bangor.

Ralph Nader had never lived in the Second. He would rank behind hundreds of other environmentalists in knowledge of what had been happening in Maine's woods and rivers in the past 300 years. Yet, Nader ranks as essential background about the Second District because Nader locked in a story about industry in 1973 that neatly defined two camps. His team called their view of events a report. Commercial interests called it a screed. Titled "The Paper Plantation," the document read like an indictment of everything that had ever happened in the counties of the Second.

"Maine is poor," the Nader report announced. "Maine is corporate country — a land of seven giant pulp and paper companies imposing a one crop economy with a one crop politics which exploits the water, air, soil and people of a beautiful state."

The case for pillaging came from many angles. Seven paper companies operating in the state, each with higher gross revenues than state government. "Great rivers sullenly serving as private sewers for the mills," the report said. Pollution and hydropower dams destroying fisheries to generate cheap power for industry; a state Legislature in the pocket of the paper companies.

Muskie may have developed the federal water standards, but "The Paper Plantation" accused the senator of not ensuring that water pollution abatement rules would apply to the Oxford Paper Company mill in his hometown of Rumford.

Voters did not need to read the Nader report — and most never did — for the document to become a political demarcation line in Maine. Rival camps in place today line up around whether their partisans believe or disbelieve that commercial interests operate recklessly in the natural environment.

In the coming decades, the divide cut across more than just the environmental regulation of paper mills or factories. Proposals for an east-west highway linking more of Canada and New York state to the isolated coast of Washington County were argued in this divide. The question of whether paper companies could pivot and use some of their land to build resorts or houses got hashed through in this divide, along with countless other issues.

Nader's raiders were not on the ground for long, but they sped along the framing of an inevitable chasm. Two sides had clout now. This break point was not just political. It was economic, cultural, and communal too. The Second began its slow death as a frontier when Pope and Talbot boarded those steamships 150 years earlier. The anything-goes nature of the "what's next" industries — hydropower, textiles, shoes and, most prominently, paper, kept the small-town mechanics alive with New England respectability, even if prospects were dimmer. The Second owned a distance-from-markets disadvantage for many endeavors. Still, in legacy industries, investors saw raw materials, rough and ready locals, and labor available from Quebec and other new arrivers. The little towns that put down their first roots in the boom of lumber and clipper ships lived to see 1973.

Other forces — global trade, automation, and big-data efficiency — hit the old ways with far more powerful body blows than Nader's. Still, the composite of a Nader-type lives big across the state nerve center in Portland and in the Second — a hero to some and a pointy-headed flatlander who just called me a victim to others. In Maine, the Nader prototype is an essential foil for Trumpism.

None of this means that old-timers are dim to the reality that the good old days were not always so good. They saw paint peeling off riverside buildings from the flow of industrial chemicals and fish species disappearing below dams, just as Muskie did. The communal divide grew because so many rural citizens are clear — even if they never heard of the "Paper Plantation" report — that a perspective casting them as victims or uninformed suckers deserves no oxygen.

The early-1970s matters because this is when any possibility for the Second to keep its frontier mentality and subsistence-living style dies. The industrial era that never fully delivered for these Maine counties was fading, automating, or going overseas. Agriculture worked only in pockets. Sizeable shares of vacationers were happier crawling like ants on popsicles at Disney or flying to Sandals Resorts than exploring the vast waters and forests inside Maine.

With those setbacks, the Information Age, just like the Industrial Age economy, took the most talented and ambitious youth away from rural counties, usually for good.

Fifty years on from the early '70s, an unspoken question is still not getting asked or sorted out in the counties of the Second: If we're not a frontier and we're not close enough to Portland or Boston to be their suburb, what are we? The natural environment is enviable enough to draw visits from every corner of the world. Yet, people who live in the vast Second are losing their grip on their places. The puzzle is not why did 51 percent of them vote for Donald Trump in 2016. The puzzle is why they did not make a louder sound sooner.

11

LYNDON AND WILBUR

"In Maine (as is true for much of rural America), health care facilities have, for all practical purposes, become the new mills — the one reliable source of continuing employment."
Charles Lawton, a Maine economist

The American political story of health care is rooted with politicians who cared about constituents in places like the rural Second.

President Lyndon Johnson's vision in 1965 was to deliver health care to elderly Americans isolated in places like his Texas Hill Country. Just as Roosevelt had extended rural electrification and Social Security, Johnson aimed to extend medical care to older citizens.

Johnson knew the political backstory. Medical services for everyone was a road not traveled by the United States when other nations turned that way. President Franklin Roosevelt stepped back from promoting universal medical insurance, fearing that opposition to it from the American Medical Association could cost him support for something he saw as more essential, Social Security pensions. President Harry Truman tried and could not extend medical coverage, brushed back by the same concern that his was a step to socialism, certain to limit what doctors could charge and stymie care for everyone.

Johnson did not go for universal coverage. Instead, he broke through in 1965 with his focus on the elderly. In the Legislative sausage-making to get it done something even Johnson likely never imagined got born — an economic base for places like the Second more important than traditional industries like paper.

Johnson passed Medicare and Medicaid. Medicare grew from the roots of Social Security, using a payroll tax to provide pension income to older

Americans. Medicare, with a new payroll tax all its own, funded hospital care for older Americans.

Medicaid — health care for the poor — was a smaller and less-noticed initiative. It had different forebears than brawny, well-rooted Social Security. Medicaid's predecessors were local hospital charity care and federally funded relief that responded to the Great Depression.

Medicaid got no payroll tax for support because it was charity. In ways logical to politicians, Medicaid was constituent service. The initiative aided people in need and, just as crucially, bridged gaps for hometown service clubs, local hospital boards of directors, and churches that helped the poor and could not sustain a modern approach to medical or social needs without investment. Medicaid, tiny at the start, opened the door to a new way to help poor people that advanced beyond person-to-person or church-to-person charity and could encompass modern medicine and social welfare.

Both Medicare and Medicaid got built into a giant revamping called the Social Security Act of 1965. Many political hairs got split to pass the legislation. Wilbur Mills, the powerful Democratic chair of the House Ways and Means Committee, was concerned that the cost of Medicare could drag down Social Security. Others worried that a narrow approach with Medicare — for example, covering only hospital care — would be dissatisfying to older Americans who stayed on the hook to pay their doctors. The idea that all of it amounted to socialism — Truman's stall point — flavored objections too.

In the end game, Johnson and Mills overcame the various objections with even bigger changes to health and welfare policy than they had imagined at the start. Addressing Mills' concern that bigger payroll taxes could become unpopular and potentially harm the bedrock popularity of Social Security, the legislation funded doctors services' under Medicare, and all of Medicaid, through the federal government's general revenue, not payroll taxes. The focus was on the elderly and the indigent, keeping the employer-based model for the workforce that doctors, employers and unions favored.

The design of Medicaid gave states the option to participate and get federal money, or not. It also gave states a say in what kind of health and welfare to support. Those two elements evaded the socialist tag. Doctors liked that Medicare kept a fee-for-service structure, which looking back many critics would see as a root cause of medical service inflation.

The medical establishment also was more comfortable with a Medicaid initiative that was an evolution from things they had seen before, like charity care, and that they could influence at the state level. Medicaid got eclipsed, too, because Medicare was the behemoth — Social Security 2.0 for older Americans and Johnson's once-in-a-generation addition to what Roosevelt had built.

What few noticed then — and what most people other than state capitol lobbyists still miss today — is how much Medicaid would come to dominate state politics and policy. Especially in small states like Maine with modest resources, Medicaid is the sun — center of the policy universe, presenting what is often the largest pot of federal money available to states and the one pot state legislators can influence in budget-making year after year. The political planets in nearly all Maine legislative sessions revolve around the state Medicaid plan.

The economies of places like the Second came to rely on health infrastructure built upon these two public health care initiatives. Medicare spending in the counties of the Second is $1.2 billion. Medicaid — which includes health, social service, and contributes to nursing home care — is more than $1 billion. These sources started from a base of zero in the late 1960s and now are essential underpinnings to the rural Maine economy. Just above 22 percent of the state's domestic product is health care — an amount above $12 billion and growing. For perspective, the forest products industry statewide — which is broadly inclusive of paper and all products generated from 17 million acres — counts its total economic impact at $8.5 billion. The counties of the Second also are obviously more dependent on health care — and public health care spending — than southern Maine. Among the top ten employers in Maine, only two are in the Second District. Both are hospitals.

Lobster fishing and paper-manufacturing are the industries that get the most attention in the Second. Lobster-fishing because it is iconic. Paper because, even with mill closures caused by market changes and automation, the six mills operating in the Second today are small-town job anchors. The less-noticed reality is that health care dwarfs both these industries. Without the public health care spending that Lyndon Johnson and Wilbur Mills birthed in 1965, the Second would be a pine-covered desert, not capable of sustaining economic or civic life.

12

JOE HENNESSEY

"On a few occasions I worked double shifts, slept in my '60 Ford Galaxie (Dave's old car) for an hour or so before school, then slept through periods five and six in the nurse's cubicle after lunch."

Author Stephen King,
recalling his schedule at a Maine mill during high school

Joe Hennessey presents like a technocrat.

He is young, fit, wearing a solid, cranberry-colored tie and a neat beard. He talks about his profession with the depth of a chemical engineer, which he is not. He understands systems. How one thing affects the next. He uses words precisely like a poet, which he also is not.

Hennessey is better at his job than 99 percent of other people are at theirs. He does not say this. You talk to others, and they tell you, and then you watch it happen. Hennessey is, as he puts it, "a teacher of English literature." He matters to the Second because Joe — friends call him Joe and students and other teachers call him Mr. Hennessey — represents a century or so of people who have done more to keep the communities of the Second together and productive than any others. Joe Hennessey is a public-school teacher.

Rural schools here have leaned into the headwinds of economic decline and uncertainty longer than other American places. Their achievement is invisible. You must sidetrack to the terrain of economics and sociology to see its shape. Then, visit with Hennessey, or peers in rural places that rarely catch a break, to see skill keeping a harsh world in better order.

The national high school graduation rate is at an all-time high, just under 85 percent. The rate at Piscataquis Community High School, where Hennessey teaches, is always above that mark, usually between 86 and 93 percent. It — and essentially every school in the Second — has maintained that lead for decades. No matter that fewer parents have college degrees compared to other places. No matter that the typical parent makes $26,000 a year, in mountain terrain where if you do not have reliable snow tires sudden death is the winter landscape's way of saying good morning.

The counties of the Second are short-circuited frontiers. Stubbornly, their school and social health is better than any reasonable oddsmaker would predict. The Robert Wood Johnson Foundation reports health and well-being outcomes across many factors. The information allows comparison to "peer counties" — places that are more alike on aspects like income and rural character. Viewed from this perspective, the counties of the Second are healthier than their peers. For example, Aroostook and Oxford counties — two bookends in the geographic span of the Second — are considered peers. Both are better off than their peer counties in the U.S. Both had the lowest numbers of premature deaths in comparison to seven peers, one in Kentucky, one in Illinois, three in Florida, and two in Alabama. Both had the lowest rate of low-birth-weight babies; the lowest teen birth rate; and the lowest child poverty rate. The counties also had substantially lower rates of violent crime in comparison to all but one peer county.

All counties in the Second have pulled off this same trick, doing better to one degree or another than cold facts should allow. The Second cannot match the health and wealth of its neighbors in southern Maine or its former Colonial protector, Massachusetts. So, seen from southern New England, the place looks beleaguered. Move the lens to a more reasonable perspective and the Second becomes an over-achiever. The glaring social fact is that residents here are older. The gap with national averages for age sticks because characters like Hennessey are the latest teacher generation readying the young for what is next, usually an endeavor outside the home county. Horrible epidemics from the outside — like opioids — take lives, but most of the kids are alright, even if they are moving to Portland, Bangor, or farther.

The immediate high school hometown of Hennessey and his colleagues — Guilford — is a unique throwback to what was more typical in small-town Maine 50 or 70 years ago. Traditional factory work is readily available right in town at two hardwood product-makers. The signs are up. They are hiring. Hardwood Products makes disposable ice cream sticks, stirring sticks, and skewers. Puritan Medical Products makes single-use medical items like tongue depressors in Guilford. The jobs are shift work, including overnights, lean in pay, and with some, not many, paths to management. The mills are respected in town. They are long-standing. They make investments in new equipment. They offer employment beyond retail jobs at Family Dollar or Walgreen's. Dozens of small towns in the region do not have anything like a Hardwood Products and so, those towns do not have a gas station or much in the way of retail stores.

The high school is a respected anchor in Guilford too. People here are not sociologists or economists, but they know that graduating nearly all the kids when three-quarters are poor enough to qualify for free or reduced school lunch is an earned thing. Principal John Keane drives the circuit of six towns spread in a 16-mile circle to fetch students who miss the bus for any reason.

"My colleagues work incredibly hard," Hennessey says.

As he says this, two or three students are poking around his classroom door, waiting for a visitor to leave so they can visit with Mr. Hennessey. He is a magnet. At first, this strikes odd. Hennessey is a formal guy who earned his degree in humanities from the University of Colorado with high honors. He says things like "in the age of acceleration, like Thomas Friedman spoke about and others have commented on, people are going to change jobs a lot more quickly." He speaks with logic and precision about a strategy at the high school — ensuring that all students have a work-ready credential, such as emergency medical technician or commercial truck driver, both a path and a high school diploma when they leave this school.

All this is sound, adult-to-adult commentary. It does not explain teenagers lining up at the door. Then, Hennessey pivots to a story about a student from three years ago who worked at Hardwood Products during high school and works there now.

"He had significant barriers to accessing his education — a chaotic home life that was probably a product of destabilization, generational poverty, all that kind of stuff," Hennessey backgrounds. "He has managed to make a good living at the mill and he also has this passion for architecture. He loves learning about it. He so willingly went above and beyond in his assignments to explore architecture and the beauty of the structure and the history of it. In particular, he loved the work of the Zaha Hadid, an Iraqi architect."

The reflection reveals the teacher. Hennessey is fiercely trying. He is listening with one intention, to make lives better. The young faces at the door have figured this out.

"You do not have to do one thing to the exclusion of all else," Hennessey says. "I think cultivating the whole person is what we do at this school."

Piscataquis Community High will keep at it, though possibly not here. The high school has entered itself in a state challenge to consolidate three regional high schools into one. Piscataquis enrolled 350 in 1990; today, only 150. Something must give. Fewer state dollars flow to the smaller pool of students, making a complete high school impossible to sustain. Principal Keane is leading the effort to merge with others, a scary leap for the community and the school. There are no guarantees that a new, comprehensive high school will get located in Guilford.

Storied thinkers and writers, artists and industrialists, and politicians have flowed through the counties of the Second. The teachers go unnoticed. They are constants, the leaders. They have stood this ground the longest.

CHASING MAINE'S SECOND

PART THREE

On the Trail

CHASING MAINE'S SECOND

MUD SEASON

"A skillful actor will make you think, but a skillful politician will make you never have to think."
Donna Brazile, political strategist

The slog for the Second gets serious for Democrats in mud season 2018 — a season other places call spring, rebranded in Maine for the ooze when mountain snow releases unreasoning water to streams, ditches, roads, and dooryards.

Democrats are choosing their congressional candidate — a reveal to their mood and a test of whether a grand vision for the Second's land can outflank passion for forcing President Trump to live with a Democratic Congress.

Jared Golden, a Marine who served in Afghanistan and Iraq, is the favorite of party insiders focused on the magic number of 23 seat gains to take control of the U.S. House of Representatives.

Two small-business owners, Tim Rich and Craig Olson, are in as independent-minded Democrats; both with passion for affordable health care. Rich believes party insiders are putting their thumb on the primary scale for Golden and signals his frustration. Jonathan Fulford, a carpenter and a hard-luck candidate for state Senate in recent years is in the mix too.

The fifth candidate, Lucas St. Clair, is the only one who could upset the bets on Golden. St. Clair is the son of Burt's Bees cosmetics millionaire and land-preservation philanthropist Roxanne Quimby. Acolytes of preservation began gathering parity with the forest products industry around time of the "Paper Plantation" report in 1973. Three decades later, Quimby became a human flashpoint in the division that emerged — between traditionalists, focused on such land uses as forest industries and hunting, and environmentalists, focused on land preservation and their vision of recreation.

St. Clair's connection to land preservation gives him a potential base of environmental voters, valuable in any Democratic primary. This makes St. Clair irksome to Democratic Party insiders because he could win the primary. He is tantalizing to some of them as well. St. Clair could be a self-funded candidate — meaning he might use gobs of that Burt's Bees fortune to fund campaign ads, were he to be the general election candidate. This outcome would sacrifice the benefit of Golden's Marine service contrasting with Rep. Poliquin. There is chatter that some national Democratic strategists are tempted at the prospect of family money freeing the donation pool to chase congressional seats elsewhere. St. Clair is not the best bet to win a general election, and yet, he is a potential bargain for strategists looking at maps bigger than the Second.

Understanding the primary contest between Golden and St. Clair requires a rollicking side trip into the life of St. Clair's mother, Roxanne Quimby. It is a tale that illuminates the experience of the Second's rural residents too — a stew of stubbornness, subsistence, and unanswered questions about how a truncated frontier can make a go of it in the Information Age.

Roxanne Quimby arrived in Guilford in 1975 with firm intent to live simply. She was a back-to-the-lander, a movement of the late 1960s and early 1970s inspired by homesteaders Scott and Helen Nearing. Quimby had other heroes, too, like Henry David Thoreau.

Quimby met her then-husband, George St. Clair, when both were undergraduates at the University of Massachusetts. They moved to San Francisco in the early 1970s, where Roxanne studied fine arts at the San Francisco Institute of Art. They had $3,000 when they began chasing their back-to-the-land vision. They drove east, mostly through Canada, advised to move north and away from waterfront to find land they could afford. The advice, and George's visits to Maine during his childhood, took them to Piscataquis County — a mountainous lake region deep inside the Second where Thoreau had toured and where 16,300 people lived in an area almost the size of Connecticut.

The young couple were part of a modest social trend, though not one where most participants would go the distance. Back-to-the-landers were scattered around, trying all kinds of the things to make a living. On the Maine coast, some tried lobstering — a traditional and, not always explained to outsiders, territorial business. In Stonington, there were tales of newcomer boats finding their way to the bottom of the harbor with no known cause.

That kind of hostility was unusual. Locals might call the newcomers hippies, but they were not hostile. Neighbors helped Roxanne and George build their home near Guilford, reachable only by walking trail and with no running water or electricity.

In those early years, Quimby was not an obvious suspect for sprouting a business and brand worth millions in remote Guilford. She was committed to living close to nature. She pedaled her bike to town for waitressing shifts to make some money. George worked at a local radio station. The couple's twin children — Lucas and sister Hannah — were born almost two years into the homesteading.

There were roots to Quimby's enterprise. She did not have much success selling artwork, yet neighbors noticed her knack for trading at flea markets — finding bargains and reselling items to supplement her family's meager income.

When the twins were five, Roxanne and George separated. Both stayed in the area. Quimby's experimentation in the world of flea markets and craft fairs took a turn in the 1984. She was hitchhiking to the post office when a local beekeeper, Burt Shavitz, offered a ride.

With his thick beard, Shavitz appeared to outsiders to have multigenerational Maine roots. He did not. In 1970, he had abandoned New York City and stringing as a photographer for Time and Life magazines, landing in Parkman, a Piscataquis County farm town fragile since its first exodus of farmers in the 1800s.

Burt practiced a subsistence living like Quimby. His steady gig was selling honey in recycled one-quart jars to neighbors. Quimby suggested smaller containers and sales at craft fairs with higher margins. A neighbor, she started helping with the beekeeping too. Decades of beeswax from Burt's farm invited product development. Quimby started with candles, experimenting freely, and found her way to skin care.

There were years, and much trial and error, and by 1990 Quimby had busted out of making candles in rural trailers and bought an empty turn-of-the-century dry goods store in Guilford for production. Her early name at craft fairs, "Electra Make Peace," was long gone. This business was Burt's Bees. A university business professor estimated its 1990 value at $106,000. Quimby borrowed a 14-year-old math-team star from Piscataquis Community High School to help keep the books. There were no idle CPAs in the woods.

Quimby's artistic and business instincts had concocted a ground-floor player in a new space — natural products and cosmetics. Shops like Zona and Bendel's in New York City were breakthrough customers.

As the leaps sprang higher, the remote Maine birthplace got left behind. Quimby told author Phyllis Austin that she reached out to the Maine Department of Economic Development when she began to outgrow the space in Guilford. By the time they reached back, she already had toured several facilities in North Carolina for her 50-employee business. Fewer financial incentives from Maine and a map that put North Carolina between market contacts and supply chains — not in a northern corner above all of it — hurt the potential for Guilford, Bangor or, outside the Second, Portland, to ride the next wave of growth for Burt's Bees.

In 1993, Piscataquis exported some of its workers to the new North Carolina home. By 1998, Burt's Bees was doing $8.2 million in sales. In 2003, a private equity firm paid $185 million for the company, with Quimby continuing to own 20 percent. Four years later, consumer products giant Clorox bought Burt's Bee's for just under $1 billion.

Missing out on a cosmetics company was not the sore point with rural Maine. Weirdly, it was a form of investment — not disinvestment — that stirred the hive here. Quimby had come into at least tens of millions, and likely hundreds of millions of dollars, at a time when huge swaths of the Maine woods were coming onto the commercial real estate market. Paper companies were selling land for the first time in decades. This was an evolution from holding the land to produce pulp, paper, or lumber to viewing the land as a tradable asset. Land integrated into a handful of companies, a factor excoriated in the "Paper Plantation" report, began to disintegrate to diverse players — some betting on the long-term value of an automated forest products industry or mixing those traditional uses with potential new uses, including development and recreation. Land conservationists and wealthy people seeking "empire lots" got into the mix.

Roxanne Quimby had a vision — common to others who had read Thoreau's The Maine Woods. She would buy and attempt to donate land for a national park in the Second's interior, making forever wild an area protected by the existing Baxter State Park and encompassing a broad area where Thoreau traveled in the 1840s and 1850s.

A group called RESTORE the North Woods, with backing from national environmental groups, including some based in Boston, advocated a park before Quimby. That inspired bumper stickers in rural Maine that said: "Restore Boston: Leave the Maine Woods Alone."

Local people saw change to their recreation and to their livelihood. Paper companies generally had been liberal in allowing hunting, snowmobiling and all-terrain vehicle riding on their lands. Some employees had leases or generations-long understandings that allowed them to put camps or cabins on lakeside property the companies owned, at little or no cost. The new conservation-oriented owners were less likely to play ball with any of that and, though less noticed, the corporate owners also were modernizing their management and tightening screws on what could be allowed.

With livelihoods, the fear was that conservationists would squeeze so much land out of service that all wood-reliant jobs — in sawmills, pulp- and paper-manufacturing, or making products from wood — were goners. The most dramatic park plans had little political traction and, even if some version of those plans came to pass, there still was a massive volume of mature or maturing trees that a new diversity of owners surely would continue to harvest. There was too much economic value — and too much land — for all forestry to stop. On the flip side, to say that locals were worrying for nothing did not add up. The woods economy was changing. The future was uncertain. Quimby became a symbol of that uncertainty, and in 2012 she saw that and exited from publicly making her family foundation's case for the economic benefits of a national park in the North Woods.

The new point person for the effort became Lucas St. Clair, Quimby's then 34-year-old son and board member of the Quimby Family Foundation. Their park vision — much smaller than what RESTORE had advocated — was not without allies on the ground. Operators of recreation-related businesses like white-water rafting and lodges would benefit from having a park destination in the region. The interior of the Second lived an ironic twist: National parks yielding economic benefits in other states had been inspired by readers of Thoreau's The Maine Woods, yet the vast interior of Maine had no national park and its impressive state park, Baxter with Mount Katahdin, was mainly a regional draw for the most dedicated hikers.

St. Clair let the wounds heal from his mother's initial relationship with the much despised RESTORE group and a disastrous 2011 interview with Forbes magazine in which she echoed the patronizing premises of Nader's "Paper Plantation" report. Quimby said her opponents were in "complete denial" about the transition of land from paper companies to new owners and that they were living in "a welfare state."

St. Clair rebuilt alliances with recreational users of the land. He became the face of the Quimby vision when it had its breakthrough success — something still controversial among traditionalists but gaining support with time. In 2016, President Barack Obama declared an 87,000-acre preserve centered around the East Branch of the Penobscot River and about one hour from Bangor to be the Katahdin Woods and Waters National Monument. Roxanne Quimby contributed land valued at $60 million and $20 million to fund the forestland management by the National Park Service.

The monument designation did not require the congressional approval that a national park needed, important because that support was not there. The Maine delegation was negative to lukewarm on the various park scenarios floated over the years. Rep. Poliquin was the most consistently opposed.

In the park effort, state media already positioned St. Clair as more reasonable and likable than his mother. The controversies related to her land purchases and the threat many felt from her vision were serious negatives for St. Clair if he reached a general election, but in a Democratic primary, where engaged environmentalists were likely voters, no one was going to attack St. Clair for being part of contributing $80 million to preserve wilderness.

Primaries attract only about 45,000 voters. If St. Clair can peel away Democrats with environmental leanings, he has a shot. In campaign forums, the style contrast between St. Clair and Golden shouts through. St. Clair looks comfortable — tall with a neatly trimmed beard and the casual "good morning" of a friendly day hiker. Golden is serious, scrubbed Marine clean, and with a light frame for uphill running. Above all, Golden is cautious. He might smirk or shrug a shoulder unpredictably, but Golden rarely says words that open doors to trouble. If he starts a wrong way, he stops. He never lets pride in his presentation get in the way of course correcting.

St. Clair is the opposite. He waxes. At a Belfast candidate forum, he goes on about how his grandfather taught him to shoot a gun. When he hits multiple notes around hunting being a male domain — a heritage "passed from fathers to sons" and "sportsmen and the use of guns go hand-in-hand" — the crowd quietly prods that women hunt too.

"And grandmothers and granddaughters to women," St. Clair adds awkwardly.

Then, his pride gets in the way and he digs the hole deeper: "My twin sister didn't take to shooting our 16-gauge shotgun the same way I did."

That is a tiny bump. Real injury comes a month before the primary with what looked like a good development for St. Clair — a group called the Maine Outdoor Alliance places TV ads touting his work to create the Katahdin Woods and Waters National Monument. The Bangor Daily News newspaper soon reports that a high school classmate who had been the best man at St. Clair's wedding had recently incorporated the Outdoor Alliance. The group declares itself a "social welfare" organization in nonprofit incorporation filings, a status that allows it to broadcast issue ads without disclosing its donors. This advances a premise that the new group is a shell — designed to tout St. Clair without transparency about where the money for this effort comes from.

No one raises their hand as a funder of Maine Outdoor Alliance. Statewide media report that one firm involved in placing the ads has done work for

Roxanne Quimby in the past. St. Clair denies any involvement in the ads. Quimby and the founder of the group do not respond to questions about the group. The controversy about who funded Outdoor Alliance ads stalls St. Clair's momentum.

The Democratic Party's signal that Golden is the disciplined choice for winning back the Congress and blunting President Trump stays on course. Before the primary even gets going, Roll Call, the Washington-based political trade journal, lists Golden as a potential contender with whom the Democratic Congressional Campaign Committee has met. None of the other candidates who eventually compete get notice as prospects.

Golden highlights that U.S. Rep. Seth Moulton, a Marine veteran from Massachusetts, has lobbied him to make the race. Serve America, Moulton's network of veterans seeking elective office, endorses Golden. The Democratic Party committees for Androscoggin County and the city of Lewiston endorse Golden. The state party declares neutrality, but there is an undercurrent message to partisans: If you want to stick it to Trump, stick with Golden.

At least one candidate gets irked with this process. Tim Rich, café owner and primary candidate from Bar Harbor, complains that "there is no nobility in losing a rigged game" and drops out three months before the June primary. "It's money. It's all money. Big money in politics has corrupted our entire way of life," Rich says. "We all know it, but we keep electing big-money people."

On election day, ranked choice voting gets its first trial in a primary for a U.S. federal office. Golden wins an initial plurality with 46 percent to St. Clair's 39 percent. After a week of tallying second choices, Golden secures a 54 percent majority to St. Clair's 46 percent.

The mysterious source of the ads supporting St. Clair is the primary's one drama. Newspaper columnists dig at that injury more aggressively than candidates. The idea that St. Clair slipped up disguises the fact that Golden won. A state legislator from Lewiston, the second-largest city in the district, Golden began the primary as the only full-time politician in the field. Others underestimate him. He moves on to take his shot at being the first Democrat ever to beat an incumbent Republican in the Second.

14

BOOMERANGS

There is a photograph and roster of the 1971 Phillips Andover Academy football team that makes the rounds on Twitter now and again.

The roster lists hometown, height, and weight. There is only one kid from Maine. The shortest guy on the team, at five feet seven, is the kid from Maine. The lightest kid on the team — by an average of 37 pounds — is the kid from Maine. Bruce Poliquin, later a congressman, is the teenage kid from Maine.

The reason these images still bump around the internet today has nothing to do with Poliquin, though he did try to claim some love around it before one Super Bowl game; trolls flamed him mercilessly.

The reason is two guys in the front row — a squinting center from Annapolis, Maryland, named William S. Belichick, and a square-headed guard from Brookline, Massachusetts, named Ernest C. Adams. Belichick goes on to win more Super Bowls than any coach in the National Football League's history. Adams works for Belichick and has mysterious-sounding titles around research. Paranoiacs whose beloved teams lose to Belichick keep the photo alive today as evidence of deep-state-style football cheating.

Both Poliquin and his challenger in this fall's election are boomerangs — a word used in Maine for neighbor kids who go out into the world to all kinds of places, often as the "only" from Maine, and come back.

Poliquin's roots are in Lewiston and Waterville, a former mill city on the Kennebec River in central Maine. Earlier generations of his family had emigrated from Quebec. When Bruce was young, the family was well-established in Waterville. Dad, Lee, was a high school teacher; mom, Louise, was a nurse. The family lived in a modest, 1,000-square-foot house on Violette Avenue, one block from a baseball field and walking distance to a new and expanded Waterville High School. Bruce shared a bedroom with his brother Jimmy, two years older.

An uncle, Ray Cyr, remembers that Bruce was "always very smart," and as Bruce and other family members describe it, the teenage Poliquin had a specific ambition to attend Harvard University. A guidance counselor advised the family that boarding school was the path. Bruce got a scholarship to Andover and, after his freshman year at Waterville High School playing hockey and baseball, was off to Massachusetts to the elite preparatory school where George H.W. Bush, then a Houston congressman, had graduated.

In the football photo, Poliquin is smiling. He makes it to Harvard the next year, graduates with a degree in economics, and starts his career in finance at Harris Bank in Chicago.

Jared Golden grew up on a vestige of the Second's past — a dairy farm converted to a golf course in Leeds, not far from the Androscoggin River "Volvo line" and the city of Lewiston.

In a state where it can snow in October or May, golf is a business as treacherous as dairy farming. Spring Brook had been the name of the farm — and it stuck with the golf course. The small group putting the golf roots down in the late 1960s included Jared's grandfather, his mom's dad. They were pragmatists — working to create a community course that could earn respectability on the humble Maine golf scene.

When Jared was a toddler, the course hosted three consecutive Maine Open championships in the mid-1980s — cementing its transition from 1960s pasture to established, community course.

It was a family business. The Goldens lived in what had been the farmhouse. A massive and still-serviceable post-and-beam barn became the clubhouse, big enough for a small banquet.

Jared, youngest of three siblings, worked on the course. All three did, from their teens to their adult years — mostly helping their dad, Joe, keep ragweed, crabgrass, trees, and brush from overrunning the fairways.

Joe likes to point out that his wife, Jeannine, owns the place — women course owners are a rarity in the golf trade.

Work, making small talk with golfers on the course, school, and sports anchored the growing up experience of the Golden kids. Jared was a sound, not standout, student. He liked team sports — football, soccer, basketball, and baseball.

The summer between Jared's sophomore and junior years in high school, "Saving Private Ryan" topped the box office. Golden remembers the heroics of the men depicted in the Tom Hanks film leaving an impression with him.

His father remembers his youngest son giving military service some consideration during those high school years. Joe's dad had fought in the Philippines. Jeannine Golden's dad was a World War II veteran too. Still, family legacies of military service were not dinner table conversation at Spring Brook. College eclipsed the military option.

Jared Golden stayed with a comfortable choice when it came to the "what next" after high school. The University of Maine at Farmington was a 50-minute drive from Leeds, and not an academic or social stretch. Jared thought he might want to be a history teacher. Farmington was a fit for anyone committed to that path. Its teachers' college roots run so deep that the science classroom building still features a gravy boat display — a tribute to a home economics teacher from 50 years earlier who had collected a prodigious number of crystal gravy boats.

The college of 1,800 students is representative of the small public colleges in the Second — all with substantially less money than comparable peers in the other New England states. Senior citizens in Farmington walk the campus's modest, indoor track at the college most mornings. The town library and campus library are next to each other, sharing books and open to all. There was never enough money to build an exclusive campus, plus the teachers who ran Farmington just were not wired that way.

Farmington is like a comfortable pair of shoes for many Maine kids breaking into higher education. For Jared Golden, the fit did not take. He said he felt like he was spending his parents' money on a path where he did not have commitment.

A change beyond the mountain town of Farmington was in the mix too. Young Golden was a week or so into his college experience when terrorists slammed airplanes into the World Trade Center in New York, the Pentagon, and a Shanksville, Pennsylvania, field, killing 2,941 civilians and 55 military service members in Washington, D.C.

Golden completed his first year at Farmington. The following fall, he told his parents that he had been talking to a military recruiter. He kept silent on his plans until just before it was time to leave for Parris Island, South Carolina, in December. The youngest Golden had signed up to be a Marine infantryman.

The parents, who Joe acknowledges were not keen on the military idea when it came up fleetingly in high school, got no chance to object this time.

"It just completely floored us," Joe Golden told the local newspaper years later. Jeannine Golden said she "walked and walked and walked and cried and cried and cried."

15

CONGRESSMAN

At age 57, Bruce Poliquin spends $700,000 of his own money seeking the 2010 Republican nomination for Maine governor. It is his first attempt at any public office. He gets clobbered, finishing sixth in a seven-candidate field with just 5 percent of the vote.

Most would have called it quits there. But, Poliquin had two valuable traits for politics — tenacity and client relations skills.

The future congressman spends much of his career before politics with Avatar Associates, a pension manager in New York City. He becomes a managing partner and client service lead — the person guiding discussion about how Avatar creates value for its corporate pension clients.

In 1989, he marries Jane Carpenter. Bruce knew Jane going all the way back to his college summers, when he was home in Waterville from Harvard. He tells a story about the time she was running an ice cream truck and he paid for his ice cream with a check so she would see his name.

The just-married Poliquins move to Cumberland, Maine, nestled on the ocean near Portland with rolling green hills and open space that make Westport, Connecticut, look like Brooklyn. Bruce stays with Avatar, which has an important client nearby in naval ship-builder Bath Iron Works. Jane, an accomplished art conservator with national experience and degrees from the University of Pennsylvania and University of Delaware, has a studio in the new family home. The couple's son, Sam, is born a year after they settle. With both their families in Maine — Jane's dad is an art historian and founder of Colby College's art museum in Waterville — the Poliquins are living their dream.

Sixteen months later a horribly distilled cruelty disrupts the young family. Jane and her father, James Carpenter, take an ocean swim during a family vacation in Puerto Rico. A rip current pulls both from shore. They drown. Bruce Poliquin, a 38-year-old pension executive, and toddler Sammy are the new family unit. Extended family and neighbors rally to them.

Decades later, young adult Sam — a financial analyst with a major film production company in Los Angeles — recounts a warm portrait of his father to a campaign news reporter. His dad always found his way on the important stuff, even if he "wasn't that good of a cook," Sam says.

Poliquin says the loss of Jane may have made him more protective of Sam, but campaign biographies do not dwell on the tragedy. The agonizing turn is placed squarely as an example of Poliquin's steadfastness, and unconnected to another chapter nearly two decades later — Poliquin's first pursuit of elective office. Poliquin's most animated and consistent responses around why he got in the game of politics emphasize desire to put his hard nose to a task of saving the taxpayer money. He may flare a personal detail into campaign conversation to gain competitive advantage — aging parents with Medicare cards, for example — but his default position is to guard personal space.

Poliquin's failed gubernatorial bid in 2010 does open a path into politics — and one that fits his favored theme of protecting taxpayers. The insurgent winner of the governor's race, Paul LePage, sweeps into office with a Republican majority and endorses Poliquin for state treasurer. The new Republican Legislature elects Poliquin, a strong fit with his finance resume, to the job.

Poliquin declares himself an "activist treasurer" — a new animal in a state that had plenty of insider schmooze in the treasurer's job before Poliquin, but not much overt partisanship. Poliquin is different. He blogs and issues press releases about alleged fiscal abuse in state government. He is both celebrated and mocked for waving about a chunk of white-oak trim used in a publicly subsidized housing project — costly trim as the pinnacle of waste. Sometimes he has a point. Sometimes he contorts context and facts to score points.

With his new platform, Poliquin tries for a bigger job in 2012. He runs in the Republican primary for U.S. Senate, finishing second in a six-candidate field with 22 percent of the vote.

With those numbers — and with family ties but no full-time residence in the Second Congressional District — Poliquin announces for the U.S. House seat two years later. The seat opens when the incumbent, Democrat Mike Michaud, decides to challenge Paul LePage for governor. Few expect Poliquin to get traction. His competitive edge in earlier races gets so far under Republican opponent skins that there are private jabs about his wee stature and perpetual motion. Poliquin gets the last laugh. The feisty finance guy glides on the same vein of disaffection that re-elects LePage as governor. Two years later, voters in rural places like the Second and rural Pennsylvania, Michigan, and Wisconsin do the same for Donald Trump, propelling him to the presidency.

Poliquin wins re-election too. He has gone from flailing efforts that established Republican operatives mocked to representing a congressional district so loyal to incumbents that it has not bounced one from office in 101 years.

Once he's in Congress, Washington presents even more welcoming ground for Poliquin as a finance pit bull. When Wells Fargo gets called to the carpet for setting up millions of consumer checking and credit card accounts without consumer consent, Poliquin does not let the fact that he accepted a $2,500 campaign donation from the bank stop him from ear-boxing their chief executive. Before the House Financial Services Committee, Poliquin's line of questioning emphasizes that the bank's malfeasance could lead to new regulation that would hurt smaller banks and constituents in his district.

At one point, John Stumpf, chairman and CEO of the bank, mistakenly calls Poliquin "Senator."

"Congressman," Poliquin snarls. "You're asleep over there."

Poliquin mixes it up with Richard Cordray, then head of the federal Consumer Protection Bureau, at another hearing and finds a harder target.

Poliquin: "Will you explain to me, sir, so I can explain to the hardworking families I represent in western, central, northern and down-east Maine, who happen to be the most frugal, hardworking people you can possibly imagine, that can stretch a dollar further than you can ever imagine, tell me why that you have a plan to spend $215 million to renovate an office building you don't own? Now, also, if I may . . ."

Cordray: "Do you want me to answer the question or not?

Poliquin: "No, not yet. So, if I'm not mistaken, I think there's supposed to be a two-story waterfall in that building with a splash pool, and a daycare center downstairs, and a playground on the roof, is that correct? Have I got this right or do I got this wrong?"

Cordray: "So, I think you've got a number of things wrong there and, by the way, I was the state treasurer in Ohio, and I represented frugal people, just as frugal as the people you talked about in Maine, I'm sure."

Poliquin: "Terrific. Tell me how I'm wrong."

Cordray: "Number one, it's apples and oranges to talk about spending $215 million. The core construction costs, as we have said all along, are in the range of $95 to $150 million."

Poliquin: "Are you folks in an office building now?"

Cordray: "I'm trying to answer your question. Do you want me to answer your question or not?"

They go on from there. Cordray, with the savvy and scar tissue of a veteran politician, holds his own. Poliquin delights in the scrap.

Political opponents feel the edge of Poliquin's competitiveness too. One from the same political party gets his first name, Les, transformed into "less jobs." A lifelong Republican gets featured in "a book of liberals" in another Poliquin ad. Poliquin tries — often successfully — to get under opponents' skins.

When pundit Paul Begala observed that "politics is show business for ugly people" it was more than a snide remark about hook-nosed politicians. It was a roadmap to the essence of politics — a place where persistence matters way more than elegance. Successful politicians are grinders. Bruce Poliquin shoves his way into elective office with effort. He is not ready to let anyone shove him out.

16

MARINE

The Lewiston Sun Journal newspaper photographed undergraduate Jared Golden at Bates College in November 2009. Sitting on the arm of an elegant teak bench — the kind private colleges dot around campus to impress parents and donors — 27-year-old Golden holds a camouflaged backpack at his knees like a security blanket. An awkward headline offers the "what's this?" of scruffy student on leafy campus: "War veteran attending Bates has heart still in Afghanistan."

The United States had 9,700 troops, and growing, when Golden reported to boot camp seven years earlier. One month before that, at the urging of the United States and key allies, the United Nations Security Council passed a resolution urging Iraq "to comply with its disarmament obligations" or face "serious consequences."

The United States was in one war in Afghanistan, where troop levels would grow to more than 100,000, and about to initiate another war in Iraq. The 20-year-old version of that kid on the teak bench had taken himself from a track to teach history in a small town to living history in a branch of the military known as the "first to fight."

In spring 2004, Golden first deployed to Afghanistan with the 3rd Battalion of the 6th Marines. He was in Kunar Province. Tucked next to Pakistan, Kunar is among the places the U.S. searched for Osama Bin Laden. Its forbidding terrain is akin to the forested Colorado Rockies. Complex tribal loyalties and combat casualties earned the place a title as Afghanistan's "heart of darkness" among U.S. military planners.

Golden recalls boredom interrupted by fear in Kunar. He was dug into a mountainside with a handful of other Marines in his first assignment. They were backing up Green Berets hunting Al Qaeda and hoping to find Bin Laden.

There is no bravado in his description of their first combat offered to a local campaign beat reporter. Fired upon at night, the five Marines could not get a fix on where the shots were coming from. In defense, "we were shooting basically in all directions," Golden said.

He faced a closer call with a truck bomb while supporting the security of the first Afghan presidential election in the fall. Later, after a stint in the U.S., he deployed to Iraq's Al Anbar province, where insurgents targeted Marines with mortars and roadside bombs. Golden got momentary glances at a furtive enemy, firing down long alleyways and certain only that if there were a direct fight "there was no question in my mind who's going down."

His battalion fought in a mission dubbed Operation Steel Curtain to push insurgents from three cities in Al Anbar near the Syrian border. The goal was to knock out safe havens for foreign fighters entering Iraq. Golden's group of Marines fought in Husaybah, a door-to-door urban clear-out job that showcased the hard realities of the Iraq campaign — firepower against the ambiguity that winning a battle with crushing power today might not matter when insurgents drifted back months or years later.

About 2,500 U.S. Marines and 1,000 Iraqi army troops fought in Steel Curtain. When the operation ended after two weeks, the U.S. Defense Department reported 10 Marines killed; 139 insurgents killed; 256 insurgents taken prisoner.

Physicians on the ground reported 97 civilians killed in the early days of the fighting. There was dispute about whether U.S. air strikes or insurgent tactics were responsible. Col. Michael Denning of the Second Marine Division air command told news correspondents that he believed the "vast majority" of civilians were killed by insurgents with improvised bombs. Urban fighting was difficult, Denning acknowledged, but sought to make the case that "insurgents will kill civilians and try to blame us."

The Marines had done their job. The larger strategic and political questions were not in their hands. Now a corporal, Golden received the Navy and Marine Corps Achievement Medal in part for leading "his Marines in advance of the platoon, clearing the path of possible improvised explosive devices or mines and gaining an initial foothold into the city of Husaybah."

There was relief and pride when Golden returned home in 2006. His hitch with the Marines was up. He took a job at a motor home dealership, mostly cleaning and keeping the merchandise looking sharp. Joe Golden noticed that wartime experiences were not behind his son. On an Interstate-95 drive, Jared's eyes were darting to inspect the road's edges, appropriate for Anbar province and not a fit for dairy fields in Litchfield and Sabattus, Maine. Golden took a screening test and was diagnosed with post-traumatic stress associated with his military service.

Years later, Golden would acknowledge that as much as he appreciated the leadership lessons of the Marines, the college scene that did not excite him at age 19 looked better after the hard training and sleep deprivation of military life. Still, it was not clear to his family whether, or how soon, he would find a path. He was getting help through the Veteran's Administration to address post-traumatic stress. He took additional jobs, including one making pies at George's Pizza, a hangout for Golden and friends back when he played for the Leavitt High Hornets.

Golden mentioned to George Stamboules, the shop's owner, that he was interested in maybe seeing if he could get into nearby Bates College, a nationally competitive liberal arts college. George knew the right guy. Bill Hiss, the admissions director at Bates, was a regular customer.

Hiss was not just any admissions director. In a decades-long career, he had been a national pioneer in breaking monolithic models of admission that relied too heavily on College Board testing. The next time he was at the pizza shop, George introduced Hiss to an ex-Marine wearing an apron. After they talked again, Hiss wrote a recommendation letter. Bates, a college founded by abolitionists in 1855, admitted Golden. The campus did not lack eager 18- and

19-year-olds. Other than Golden, Bates had no one who had taken a path to this secure terrarium through Kunar province and Husaybah.

STRATEGY

What Golden described as "a chance encounter and some good luck" got him to Bates. Once there, he had the chance to reflect on his experiences in Afghanistan and Iraq and, at times, be the voice giving military context to what peer undergraduates saw on cable news as certain outrages.

Wars are political. Golden kept his academic major in history and added a new one in politics.

Even in those undergraduate days, Golden took care in how he discussed Afghanistan and Iraq. He wrestled with the ambiguity of both places and seemed to have more hope for and investment in Afghanistan. "I can't tell people what's necessarily right or wrong in Afghanistan," Golden told a Bates College newsletter in 2010. "I'm just trying to go there and find ways to make a small difference."

Golden returned to Kabul, Afghanistan, as an undergraduate in the summer of 2009 to work at a leadership school. A foundation named for Peter M. Goodrich, a Bates College alum who died in the Sept. 11 attacks, supported the school. The following summer a role with a logistics company supporting U.S. agencies took Golden to Baghdad.

His new pedigree — Bates and the Marines — opened a door when he graduated in 2011. He got a job working for U.S. Sen. Susan Collins of Maine as a staffer on the Senate Homeland Security and Governmental Affairs Committee. Collins was a popular Republican positioned as a moderate. Golden had a junior role on what, at the time, was a less partisan committee.

Only a couple of years later, Golden was in the thick of electoral politics as a Democrat. He ran in Lewiston House District 60, the area of the city that included the downtown and, a short distance away, Bates College. He won in the safe Democratic district with 62 percent.

During the campaign Golden began dating Isobel Moiles, another Bates graduate, who was working as a regional field director for the Democratic Party's statewide campaign. Within a few months they were engaged and the summer after his election to the Legislature, Golden and Moiles were married at his family's Springbrook Golf Course, with a reception in the barn turned clubhouse. Isobel ran unopposed in November for a seat on the Lewiston City Council, representing the neighborhood near Bates where the couple bought a tiny starter home. Jared had promised in his wedding vows never to run against his wife for political office.

Golden got re-elected to another two-year term in the state House in 2016, increasing his tally to 66 percent. He earned the number three slot in the Democrat Party's legislative leadership, too — assistant majority leader.

The potential next step — the congressional seat — was one that both he and Isobel knew from direct experience was difficult, maybe impossible, to get. As a field director in the Democrats' 2014 coordinated campaign, Isobel had tried to win the seat for Emily Cain, a more experienced candidate than Golden. Cain had more responsibility as a state legislator, serving first as House minority leader and then winning election to the state Senate from Orono, home to the 11,000-student University of Maine.

Without the foil of Donald Trump in the White House, the river of campaign dollars had not flowed so easily to Cain's door. It did not matter. Cain was good at raising money. Poliquin, at that point never having been elected to anything, gave himself a $122,000 donation in 2014. He still could not keep up with Cain, who raised just under $2 million compared to his $1.7 million.

With that — and the chance to face Poliquin when he was not the incumbent — Cain lost in 2014. She tried again in 2016. She out-raised incumbent Poliquin $3.5 million to $3.4 million. She lost again.

In Cain's experience there were lessons about the Second. Lessons, too, about just how fickle politics can be.

Cain was not a native. Her family moved a few times when she was young. She graduated from high school in New Jersey before attending the University of Maine. The roots she put down were at the university — her first job after college was there. She was identified with the Legislature and the university, not a home region. None of that was disqualifying, but the best resume for being "from away" in the Second is a great-grandmother from Quebec, not a mom from New Jersey.

Golden could hope that Cain had been the victim of bad timing too. The attempt at the open seat came in 2014 — an off-year election for President Barack Obama. Off years are famously bad for candidates whose party holds the White House. In Maine, 2014 also was the year when Maine Democrats stumbled trying to unseat Republican Gov. Paul LePage.

The try to knock out Poliquin in 2016 came in the same year that small-town voters sharing some common experiences with the Second — rural Michigan, Wisconsin, and Pennsylvania — were paving a road for Donald Trump to triumph. Those voters understood instinctively that politics was not their sport. Trump was their proxy to blow up the game.

Golden had easy money from frustrated Democrats and alarmed independents in 2018. He could hope, too, that even those who wanted to change the game may have acquired some pause about burning down the stadium. He could hope that his timing was better.

History offered the former Marine little hope. In fact, it was poised to crush him. Two years earlier, only 3 percent of challengers won congressional seats. Those odds were favorable compared to the Second District, which routinely tossed new political faces overboard like seaweed raised with a trap line. A challenger had not beaten an incumbent congressman here since 1916 — when Republican Wallace White beat Congressman Daniel McGillicuddy, a Democrat from Lewiston. No Democrat had never beaten an incumbent Republican in the Second.

Brent Littlefield, Poliquin's lead strategist, knew this history well. He was on familiar ground in the Second too. His greatest career successes launched two Maine politicians who few saw as prospects before Littlefield got involved. Republican LePage squeaked his narrow path to victory in the primary and general election for governor with Littlefield's help.

Poliquin enlisted Littlefield in 2014. Before Littlefield, Poliquin's election experience was consistently grim — large self-funding checks and large losses. In 2014, Poliquin and Littlefield synched. Both were aggressive and fully committed to the idea that Democrats were freeloaders with no grasp of commerce or the ways of the world. In their version of a caricatured, hyperpartisan divide, Poliquin and Littlefield saw defenders of American values and commerce when they looked in the mirror. With a career only in politics, Littlefield's life work anchored to the idea that anyone who saw even a sliver of value in a screed like "The Paper Plantation" report was not fit to govern. Well before Trump invented the catchall "fake news," both Littlefield and Poliquin were invested in a belief that those questioning power from the left were, at best, a nuisance.

Poliquin had enlisted zealous helpers before. Littlefield offered something more — a knack for choosing and framing alleged outrages in ways that sparked the disaffected to go to the polls and vote Republican. The new consultant brought out the best in Poliquin — leveraging his client skills developed during decades helping financial officers navigate pensions and his team-sport combativeness from the playing fields at Andover and Harvard.

Littlefield presented like a typical Washington, D.C., maven. He founded Littlefield Consulting there in 2008. He showed up occasionally on cable news — "the shows" in Trump lingo — to bat about the issues of the day.

Closer inspection showed that Littlefield was the only strategist in the 2018 race born and educated in the Second. He grew up in Winn, a town in remote Penobscot County where the population peaked in 1890 at 900. The Boston-owned tannery burned down in 1893; 400 people live in Winn now.

Littlefield grew his political teeth in Maine. He majored in political science at the University of Maine, chaired the College Republicans, and did battle in student government with Ethan Strimling, a kid from New York City who later became the liberal mayor of Portland.

Littlefield worked in junior political positions for Maine Gov. John "Jock" McKernan and then led the unsuccessful re-election bid for a First District Republican, Jim Longley. Later, he smartly put himself where his industry —

politics — was booming, Washington. Littlefield was another son of the Second exported. He boomeranged back only for family visits and to win elections.

The Golden campaign collected senior staffers with military backgrounds and limited Maine experience.

Jon Breed, the campaign manager, had worked for a D.C. trade association and served as a naval officer, specialized in submarine warfare. Bobby Reynolds came on board as campaign communications director from Main Street Solutions, the lobbying shop of Portland law firm Verrill Dana. Main Street had good Bangor political roots. Like Breed, Reynolds got his start serving in the Navy.

The Golden campaign also engaged an array of experienced Washington service firms — experienced pollsters like The Mellman Group and experts in media buying and advertising production. Like Poliquin, the candidate was not disengaged from political strategy. His state House district may have been safe, but he was proud of winning two races there with healthy margins.

Money and layers of help were not the only parallel attributes of the Golden and Poliquin campaigns. Their strategies were calculated and conventional. Neither candidate, nor supporting cast, was likely to break new political ground or tout novel policy solutions.

Poliquin cagily kept a distance from Trump, never criticizing the president and never acknowledging whether he voted for Trump or not. Second District voters were not a perfect Trump fit. They liked using him as a device to stick it to the pointy-headed experts. On the other hand, Trump's Manhattan via Queens via Deutsche Bank bullshit was about as far from the Second's work reality as one could travel. Poliquin instinctively walked a tricky line to keep a separation from Trump that was as much cultural as political.

The core of the Poliquin re-election strategy was to lean into constituent service narratives and to try to disqualify the other guy as a leftist. The fundamentals common to both sides: Say things that will motivate your voters to vote; avoid saying things that could energize the other side's voters; when possible, make the other guy unacceptable to that narrow band of voters who had not made up their minds. Team Golden would hammer away at their candidate's biography of service and the issue of health care access — looking to immunize from attacks, energize their voters, and make Poliquin look slippery. Their first long-form ad from the primary season die-cast a message of Marine as reliable change-agent that underpinned their enterprise.

The ad opens in a quiescent Maine harbor. Two lobster boats glide past in thin mist, beginning their workday. In the same predawn light, you see a young man with a military-style haircut running on rural hardtop. His T-shirt is emblazoned with a saying attributed to Chesty Puller, legendary U.S. Marine and World War II battlefield leader: "Pain is weakness leaving the body." Over this image, district voters hear Golden's voice for the first time. "I'll never forget what it felt like running across the field and up the ridgeline to the sound of gunfire," he says. "On the other side of that ridge, three of our Marines were in a firefight. We were racing to get there faster because they needed us to have their backs. We knew they'd have done the same for us. That's just what Marines do."

The images pivot to the hometowns of the Second. Panning above Lewiston's Androscoggin River and Bangor's campy Paul Bunyan statue, then turning to portraits of constituents and symbols of the region: Franklin Memorial Hospital in Farmington, the shuttered paper mills of Millinocket, the long-vacated factories of Lewiston. Congressman Bruce Poliquin makes an appearance in fuzzy phone-camera video. The same images had made the local news — the congressman exiting a gathering to avoid a confrontational question about health insurance.

Golden's voice-over frames his story around these images — good people not served by Washington, special interests, and Poliquin. All in contrast to the reliability of Marines who served in Afghanistan and Iraq.

"We need leaders who are as tough as we are," Golden concludes. "I'm Jared Golden and I am running for Congress. I'll give you my word. I'll always have your back."

Congressman Poliquin had incumbency and history on his side, and plenty to worry about.

SKIRMISH

"Spring is a little desperate. Winter can be too, if you are not used to winter. Summer looks pretty sweet."
John Wentworth, Monson, Maine

Pity for the Second is foolish, most obviously in August.

Every corner of the north country conjures paradise in summer. Levitation-worthy conditions — full sun, a world of fresh water, and starry nights — prevail. The marketed ocean does its craggy coast, clam bake, sail-powered thing. Inland, the rivers, lakes, and mountains twirl their magic. They have extraterrestrials called moose — obtuse, big deer cousins with lingering legs tinker-toyed to Winnebago-sized bodies, and outnumbering people in some parts. Summer is weird, warm, and wild. An unchilled beer is about as difficult as it can get.

Leaving the television off, and not being reckless enough to let a major political party into your social media feed, is required this summer to avoid a different kind of August downer. Thirty-one million in campaign dollars are at work.

Team Poliquin bids to scrape shine off their challenger. The most prominent pro-Poliquin ad out of the gate plays offense on health care, the trickiest topic for the congressman. Poliquin's ad works to sow doubt that Golden's ideas about health care are "too radical and too risky." Golden's "health-care scheme" would cost "$32.6 trillion," the ad says. The pitch to those with health care — in particular, seniors with Medicare — is that the new guy will mess up what you have.

There are precious few large, private employers in the counties of the Second. In fact, the only two organizations here to crack the list of the state's top-ten employers are both hospitals. This economic profile makes finding employer-provided health insurance in the rural terrain tough. The district's aging population gets caught between not being old enough to qualify for publicly funded Medicare and not having access to reliable or affordable private insurance. The Affordable Care Act — or Obamacare — is not established enough or simple enough to be wildly popular here. Still, its provisions around enforcing continuity of coverage, protecting people with pre-existing conditions, and enabling some adult children to stay on their parents' health insurance are valued.

Poliquin backs private market health care. His base of partisans is even more vocal in their philosophical stance to repeal Obamacare. The congressman took heat from this base in 2014 when one of his first votes in Congress went against a repeal of Obamacare. Since then, he has consistently voted to repeal, saying the later bills were paired with plans to replace Obamacare and protect access. Those plans are not spelled out in legislation, so there is fog around the safe harbor Poliquin offers. He is caught between multiple votes seen as taking health care access away from his constituents and a single, early vote that went the other way and makes the partisan Republicans he needs suspicious.

Making matters worse for Poliquin, his challenger backs extending Medicare to people older than 55, creating another path of health care access for constituents. The congressman's ad tries to put Golden on the defensive around health care to reverse what is happening to him.

Golden takes a ride on a lobster boat in his August ad buy. "It is time for Maine to show Washington what needs to go overboard," the candidate says, holding a fistful of seaweed. Then, he slides a lobster trap into the drink as he rattles off what must go: "partisan politics, since we're all part of the same team; special interests that block cheaper prescription drugs from Canada; and, career politicians like Bruce Poliquin who voted for plans that would gut Social Security and Medicare."

The ad is clunky, poll-tested groupthink. Golden holds up a lobster at the end and says, "We have to throw out what's bad with Washington and get something good."

These ads begin a season of skirmishing that heats above the typical Maine campaign temperature.

Golden finds a counterpunch on health care in a column from George Smith, a Republican congressional staffer from back in the 1970s who is better known as a former executive director of the Sportsman's Alliance of Maine.

"It was particularly wrong for Poliquin to attack Golden on health care issues, given that Poliquin voted to repeal the Affordable Care Act, which would have stripped tens of thousands of Mainers of their health insurance. Thankfully Sens. Angus King and Susan Collins helped block that move in the Senate," Smith writes.

The next wave of summer heat comes when the state Republican Party tries to create suspicions about Golden's military commitment. They poke into the archives of a Bates College magazine and find undergraduate Golden and a student from Afghanistan speaking about how they dealt with stereotyped views of both Afghans and Americans among their peers on campus.

"Get as many different perspectives as possible. Don't just jump on a bandwagon or make assumptions," Golden says in the magazine. "I really always try to paint the picture from both angles. I can see Afghans who do appreciate our being there, who feel better that the Taliban no longer runs their area or who love the fact that their child is going to school. And I can also see that that same family has lost five or six family members to U.S. air support."

This was hardly the stuff of campaign opposition research dreams. But, a little farther on in the article was something an editor with intent could work with. In the context of saying that he is glad his Bates peers could now see him as a student and not just a Marine, Golden had said something eight years earlier that caught a political operative's eye. The exact wording in the magazine is helpful:

He adds that at Bates, "some people, I'm happy to say, don't really associate me with my military experience anymore."

The quote gets re-engineered in a Maine Republican Party Facebook post next to a photo of Golden with his Afghan classmate that removes any hint of context:

"Some people, I'm happy to say, don't really associate me with my military experience anymore."

At the same time, another surrogate to the Republican side — the Congressional Leadership Fund of House Speaker Paul Ryan — is taking a run at Golden on a novel topic: tattoos.

The earliest Golden campaign ad, and all others that followed, showed the young candidate with sleeves rolled up, revealing a tattoo on his forearm. The tattoo is a Gaelic cross, a Christian symbol with Irish roots. Team Golden may have wanted the tattoo image to reinforce their candidate's ties to military service. Their shot put the body art in a modest, "one-of-us" light.

Ryan's Fund — the highest-dollar outside group supporting Poliquin — attempts to reframe the tattoo as a symbol of recklessness. Their 30-second ad intones: "Golden voted to allow welfare recipients to use your tax dollars to buy tattoos, tobacco, alcohol, even lottery tickets." The image then switches to a close-up of the Gaelic cross on Golden's forearm and pans out to the full shot of him. The ad closes with a cartoonish image of a man's back. Golden's face is tattooed on the back, below a label, "Liberal Jared Golden," and next to the word "FREE!" The voice-over: "Liberal Jared Golden. Wasteful handouts for them. Higher taxes for us."

Team Golden — reacting to the Facebook shot and the tattoo ad — declares a Jack Nicholson moment.

"They screwed with the wrong Marine," the campaign spokesman Bobby Reynolds tells the press.

To this melodrama, team Poliquin tries to add a victim card. The image of the lobster trap metaphorically tossing Poliquin into the ocean is insensitive to the tragic drowning of Poliquin's wife, Jane Carpenter Poliquin, in 1992, they say. Reynolds for Golden says the ad has been on the air for 10 days. If it is such an obviously insensitive outrage why are we only hearing about it on the day when we are pushing a case that your side is distorting our guy's pride in his military service?

This is what $31 million buys you. It is going to be a long summer, for both campaigns. The Second and its people are not bothered. The Second is paradise right now, a time to float, fish, and eat blueberry pie. Almost no one is listening.

19

LEWISTON

"The Canadians came to the city — giving it new life, new fervors, new charms, new vivacities, lighter touches, pleasant shades of cultivation, bringing no harm to the city, bringing what it now has — a freshening of city style, a richer sense of plain living."

Artist Marsden Hartley,
a remembrance of Lewiston, Maine

Jimmy Simones sells $1 hot dogs in Lewiston. Politics talk is free at his canary-yellow counter.

This October day, Jimmy says, talk about the congressional race is paused. Everyone is chattering about whether the sexual assault allegations against Supreme Court nominee Brett Kavanaugh are true, or provable, or something else. The controversy blankets cable news. Customers echo it back.

People are noticing the volume of television ads from the congressional race, Jimmy says. No one story line from the multi-million-dollar onslaught is getting playback at breakfast or lunch. Jimmy's summation: "The ads are like, 'he said, she said, they said.' They go back and forth, contradicting each other."

In this traditional city of 32,000 people, Jimmy is a traditional guy. His grandfather started a tiny hot dog stand across the street 110 years ago. He was a Greek immigrant serving French-Canadian textile, shoe factory, and paper mill workers who had immigrated from the north. The modest restaurant that grew from his success has a dozen or so tables and busy lunch counter. "We were just named the best hot dog place in Maine by 'Peoples,' " Jimmy says.

People, the magazine, knew the joint and took measure of its personality, likely not its hot dogs. They photographed former U.S. Sen. Olympia Snowe visiting Jimmy's place in 2012. Snowe, a native of Lewiston's "twin city" of Auburn across the Androscoggin River, announced that year that "Washington is broken." She left the Senate.

Simones is bona fide community — a safe, grilled-with-only-the-grill's-seasoning place. Regulars come because the food is the same, not expensive and not memorable. The counter help, by a New England yardstick, is friendly. Non-regulars come because they divine an authentic crossroads of old-school Lewiston. Jimmy keeps a guest book. He flares with delight at its diversity of signatures — "Jerry Mathers! The Beaver!" — the semifamous, famous, and people from every corner of the world.

"Bruce Poliquin has been in, quite a few times actually," Jimmy says. "We haven't seen Golden yet. Hopefully, he'll drop in. We would like to see him. Customers would like to see him. This is a place where you can meet the candidates and ask questions."

As much as Jimmy says his place is neutral — and his photo wall of fame includes Democrats and Republicans — the television is tuned to Fox News. No question, Democrats stop in at Simones. But the potentially available voter, generally younger, is less common here. The risk-reward calculus of modern campaigns is to find and motivate your probable voters, not waste time or get trolled by locked-down preferences. Simones is not likely to see Golden before the vote.

At the counter, another candidate remembers his first political race twenty years ago. Republican Nelson Peters, Jr. says his Democratic opponent for state representative was the incumbent and his former high school math teacher. They had coffee together the afternoon of the election, then went together to city hall to see the returns come in. Peters lost. There were no hard feelings, he says. Peters is now the retired deputy police chief in Lewiston. He got asked by the Republican state Senate president this year to make a long-shot bid for the Lewiston state Senate seat.

"My wife runs a bridal shop and the only day she needs me is Wednesdays when the tuxedos come in. So, I figured, why not? I've got the time, I can run," Peters says.

He does not think he will win. He also does not expect he and the incumbent will be having coffee. This is a different time.

Strategists on both sides of the hunt for the congressional seat know that Lewiston likely will decide the Second's race. The margin is the big deal. Democrats will carry Lewiston, but it is essential for them to run up their score here to cover their weakness in rural towns.

Golden and Poliquin have strengths and gaps in their Lewiston portfolios. Golden already has won state elections in part of the city. The gap is that he is associated more with Bates College, and nearby Leeds where he grew up. He does not have French-Canadian heritage, an asset and symbol of working-class roots here.

Poliquin has that French-Canadian heritage, but he never lived in Lewiston. A bigger challenge is that opponents in all his races have pounded at an image of the former pension client manager as a leather-soled Wall Streeter, a guy from New York, or at least Portland, which is almost as bad on the cultural landscape.

So, Lewiston makes both campaigns tense. Its working-class roots feed the powerful block that Muskie organized to get the Democratic Party off its back in the 1950s. The mostly French Catholic residents of Lewiston had a century-long rivalry with Irish Catholics from Portland. Still, in 1960, Lewiston Catholics had no trouble setting aside intramural spats about Catholic schools and basilicas. The city gave the first successful Catholic candidate for president, Jack Kennedy, 72 percent of its vote. The fray in that coalition shows in Lewiston's election of Republican mayors these days. Socially conservative appeals around issues like welfare work here.

The psyche of Lewiston is defensive, and justifiably so. The city is the third largest in Maine, and the one place — city or town — most misunderstood and actively mistreated. Neighboring towns nickname it "the dirty Lew" — tagging the city for its mill-city vestiges like the industrial canal sliced into downtown.

It is common, wrong, and easy to disprove knowledge in Maine that Lewiston holds title to the state's highest crime rate. In truth, Lewiston, never cracks the top of the crime-rate list, a healthy achievement because Maine is pretty much dead last for crime in national statistics.

The bash on Lewiston has other roots too — in the sights and sounds of a four-block area downtown where social services are delivered today and in ancient prejudices against French-Canadians who arrived with nothing and large families in the 19th century to keep the factories humming at low wages. People who carry on "the dirty Lew" stereotype today do not know they are parroting sounds from an earlier era of bias, akin to stereotyping today's immigrants.

Lewiston has worked hard for generations and stayed on the short end of an economic stick that favors those farther south and on the ocean coast. Its pride is hurt. The rural towns to the north and west of the city share a similar experience, but people in those parts have no love for Lewiston either. They see it as sitting on "the Volvo line" at the Androscoggin River, more part of Portland's orbit than their frontier.

Steve Costello's family published the Lewiston Sun Journal newspaper for three generations. One of his gut reactions about Lewiston's status is that Portland — Maine's largest city and declared the spiffiest in the state by all in the know and from away — "wants to keep Lewiston down." On reflection, Costello recognizes that this is how it feels to be Lewiston, and that the reality is worse. Portland is not thinking about Lewiston at all.

The irony in this is that the migration pattern for people leaving the towns of the Second is not out-of-state for the most part; it is to the county next door. Androscoggin County, home county to Lewiston, is an exporter of people to Portland's home base, Cumberland County. U.S. Census data shows that in the most recently studied four-year span, Androscoggin County lost 346 people to Cumberland County, with about one-third leaving from Lewiston. Portland is growing with expats from Lewiston, and not acknowledging its beleaguered old rival at all.

Visiting around Lewiston you find others revealing the profile of this city — proud and earning everything they have without recognition.

Daniel Bailey profiles like the region — rooted here many generations, first on coastal Bailey Island named for his ancestors. His father dug clams and did other odd jobs as the family transitioned from working on the land to working in factory towns like Lewiston. He found a refuge in high school at Zimmie's Comics — a place for teenagers more interested in Dungeons and Dragons than Lewiston High's Blue Devils football team.

The empty storefront nature of Lewiston's downtown is such that when Bailey took out a small loan a few years ago to buy the comics business and keep its 300 square feet leased and operating, five city and county officials turned out for a ribbon-cutting. The store barely makes money. It is a community. Bailey stays open on Christmas and serves cookies to customers who are a Lewiston version of television's "Big Bang Theory" cast.

Bailey makes a point, too, of announcing, without being asked, that if the business fails, "I will work as many shifts at McDonald's as it takes to pay off the loan. That's just the way it is." Few people in the world know more about superheroes and fantasy games than Bailey and — with all that — he is New England Yankee to the core.

Over at the public library, Dianna Larrabee, in her 20s, is younger than Bailey and, like him, not too exercised about politics. She is doing one of her two jobs — as an outreach worker for Community Concepts, a social service agency. She also works at Dunkin' Donuts. One of her sisters has a good job at Dunkin', a general manager. All four siblings help take care of their mom who worked many years in a small, metal manufacturing plant and is disabled with a chronic lung disease.

Service jobs — especially in health care — are today's backbone in Lewiston and across the Second. Dianna's experience caring for someone with a disability is more common in the Second Congressional District than just about anyplace in the United States. The stunning and invisible fact about the Second is that it is an island of disability. There are 50 congressional districts in New England and New York. None of those places, or Canada to the north, have as many disabled people as the Second of Maine. Almost 120,000 of the 600,000 residents in the district are disabled.

This profile makes health care — the cost of insurance in places like Lewiston and access to hospitals and services in remote areas — the issue Golden most wants to emphasize. Republicans make headway in places like Lewiston when they can shift the focus to welfare and other so-called wedge issues, like guns.

Over at the University of Maine at Farmington, Jim Melcher, the political scientist, is watching to see if Lewiston, and the Second as a whole, is changing its political stripes. Ninety-five percent white, the Second — and Lewiston — voted for Barack Obama for president twice. That built a streak of six presidential elections in which the Second had voted for the Democratic candidate. Then, the district went for Donald Trump by 10 percent. One possibility is that Hillary Clinton was an "awful" fit with the district, Melcher says. The other is that social conservatism around topics like welfare put the district in the column of Trump Republicanism, locking Lewiston and its rural cousins into a new pattern.

National poll-crunching of Trump's win showed issues of immigration and race as wedges supporting his wins in key states. Almost 80 percent of Trump voters characterized immigration as a "very big" problem compared with only 20 percent of Clinton voters, according to Pew Research Center's surveys. Similarly, the two sides divided on whether racism was a serious problem in the country — 53 percent of Clinton voters saw it that way; only 21 percent among Trump voters did.

The talking-head assumption that "blue collar" workers ran to Trump did not hold up to inspection. Only about one-third of Trump supporters self-identified as "blue-collar." One-third of Trump's primary supporters made more than $100,000 and another third were well above national averages for median income. The more precise profile of the Trump voter is someone who has some economic standing to lose and fewer higher- education credentials.

The Second is not ideal ground for making political hay with fear of immigrants, but Lewiston is the place where a demagogue could try. In the prior two decades, the city and close-by areas like Auburn gained 7,000 African refugees, many asylum seekers from Somalia and east Africa.

The few local politicians who hint at resentments about new Mainers usually back away quickly or circle their message around concern about costs. The one politician who most directly infused the topic with fear is Donald Trump. In June 2016, candidate Trump told a rally in Maine that "we've seen many, many crimes getting worse all the time, and as Maine knows — a major destination for Somali refugees — right, am I right?"

When his implication pushed the crime question to Lewiston's police chief that afternoon, the chief pushed back: Crime had fallen 15 percent in the city during the prior year, consistent with its long-term trends.

"The Somalis come here because they want somewhere safe and good schools to raise their kids, and that's what Lewiston has," Chief Brian O'Malley told the newspapers.

It is not that everything is easy about integrating new cultures and language into Lewiston, but the city's old soul helps. French is spoken here — just as it is in parts of Somalia — a vestige of those French-Canadian emigres, most of them Catholic. Those families lived through eras when the Ku Klux Klan had fancy meeting halls in Maine's major cities and a favored topic of paranoia: Catholics. There were earlier waves of French-speaking political refugees too — the Acadians, chased out of Canada by the British, scattered to places as far-flung as Aroostook County in the far north of the Second and New Orleans.

Lewiston's most recent refugees are writing their chapter — filling a few long-vacated storefronts in the downtown and stoking school pride. Netflix has optioned a movie about some boys who first came to know each other playing soccer in a Kenyan refugee camp. Later, they came together again in Lewiston and made a promise to the long-suffering Lewiston High School soccer coach: We will make the team and we will win a championship. Lewiston, a football town, won its first high school soccer state championship ever in 2015. They won again in in 2017 and 2018, with townies in flannel and soccer moms in traditional Muslim head scarves filling the bleachers, part of a new winning tradition.

Stirring resentment in Lewiston about people who are different looks easy — especially to outsiders — but it is not an uncomplicated game. So far this fall, Poliquin is keeping a distance from the most visceral, Trumpian appeals around immigration.

20

THE INDEPENDENTS

Tyler Adkins of Monson via New York City and the Philippines is finding roads and houses among the slopes of Piscataquis County that he never knew existed. Door-to-door is a different kind of campaigning when the doors are miles apart, and up and down valleys dense with pine and rock.

Adkins is not alone journeying as a political independent in rural Maine. Independence runs thick in the Second. It is not a political party. It is a durable state of mind.

Norm Higgins is running in a neighboring legislative district around the old shoe town of Dover-Foxcroft. He had a safe gig as a Republican state representative. Then, in the fall of 2017, he put that at risk. Higgins, 70, and a former school principal at Piscataquis Community High School, unenrolled from the Republican Party.

Higgins had been the only Republican in the State House to vote for a state budget earlier in the year. It was his attempt to avert a state government shutdown. He failed. State offices and services stopped for three days before the budgeteers landed where they easily could have landed without any chaos. Higgins does not dwell on that, or any one cause or leader for his dash from the party. His frustration, building for years, is with both major parties. Both are locking down in pat positions, he says, counting only "wins and losses," and uninterested in problem-solving. Representing a place with no time for games, one desperately needing pragmatism, his instinct is to stay friendly with all political tribes and point them at opportunities to do good.

"If you are waiting for someone to come here and fix this county you will die first," Higgins says. "No one gives a crap about this place but the people who live here."

This fall, Higgins believes he is running behind in his re-election bid. He is now an independent, in a place where his re-election as a Republican would have been a lock. Lately, he is feeling more optimistic. "The Republicans at the last minute blinked and withdrew their candidate," he says.

Norman, as neighbors call him, is a fixture in Piscataquis, spectacular terrain where the Appalachian Trail turns to its destination at the summit of Mount Katahdin. He was the kind of school principal, and later school superintendent, who would make the rounds to gas stations, coffee shops, and churches to explain when a big change was coming, not hide it or pretend that a school board meeting was a comfortable venue for everyone.

The going-to-college rate at Piscataquis High sprang from 15 percent to 65 percent during Higgins' tenure there in the 1980s and '90s. With an unafraid band of teachers, he shaped a fierce legacy of higher aspiration and pragmatism that young teacher Joe Hennessey spotted all the way from Colorado. Higgins and his crew had long ago moved on when Hennessey arrived. Their stubborn commitment to students stuck to the place, even with enrollment and the dollars attached to enrollment plummeting.

Among voters, there is another side to stubborn. Rookie candidate Adkins is running into a wall of worry — joined with paralysis — as he makes his rounds in the neighboring district that includes Higgins' old high school.

People are concerned about their property taxes — specifically whether a quirky windfall of money suddenly flowing to the town of Monson can hurt them. He keeps hearing a fallacy that philanthropists investing in Monson will pay no property taxes on the remodeled buildings they are putting up in the town's center.

The 34-year-old candidate has his own concerns about these newcomers. A Portland-based foundation's vision, based on some actual Monson DNA as a place attractive to artists, intends to spur development of an arts colony. Fine with Adkins. He just wants to make sure there is a focus on broadband coverage and that local people are engaged in important choices, like zoning.

What he is hearing at the kitchen tables is not aligned with his "this is a good thing, but we need to manage it" perspective. Instead, he is seeing a paralytic fear of any change. "It's been so bad for so long that everyone is just trying to figure out how to survive," he says.

You do not easily get the complete ghost town of a western prairie in New England places like Piscataquis County. The woods economy, the trickle of summer recreators, and most substantially, public spending on health care and schools, are a floor. The decades long pattern is slow death, not actual death. Monson itself has 660 people now, down from a peak of 1,243 in 1910 when the slate quarry was busy.

Much later, in 2007, the population dipped again after Moosehead Manufacturing, a furniture maker in Monson, closed.

Moosehead won $206,000 in 2006 after leading a trade complaint against Chinese manufacturers for dumping low-cost bedroom furniture on the U.S. market. It was not enough. Owner John Wentworth told the trade publication Furniture Today that he would wind down the business in an orderly way rather than declare bankruptcy. Thirty-six workers stayed on in 2007 to complete orders; about 80 lost their jobs.

Today, Wentworth reflects on the hard facts he saw then. "Not that I'm a visionary or anything, but I could see the market changing and that it was not coming back. So, what's the sense in limping along for a year or two and then sticking a lot of suppliers and saying, 'Sorry, we're going bankrupt; we can't pay you now'? We paid everybody off."

A couple of years later, Monson Elementary School closed. Forty-two kindergartners, first-, second-, third-, and fourth-graders began taking the bus 17 miles one-way to the school in Dover-Foxcroft.

This picture of decline begs questions about why anyone would invest millions today in the crumbling, wood-frame buildings of town center Monson. Oddly, the answer makes sense. Arts scene insiders connected dots. Teeny, beleaguered Monson, they saw, owned legacy and talent in the arts.

Berenice Abbott, a world-renowned photographer, moved to Monson in the 1950s after lung surgery. She did much of her work here until her death in 1991. Todd Watts, an outstanding fine arts photographer and artist, worked for Abbott here, printing her photographs. A few years after her death, Watts relocated to the area from New York City to do his work. Jemma Gascoine, a potter from London and Todd's wife, has been making and selling art internationally from Monson for almost 20 years now. Alan Bray, a graduate of Monson Elementary School and a world-class painter, never left the area. He lives and works in nearby Sangerville.

Monson has other assets. Its main street is perched on elegant Lake Hebron, with 100-feet depth. The town lives close to the Appalachian Trail — the last town anywhere near the trail before it enters the 100-Mile Wilderness on the way to its spectacular terminus, Thoreau's Mount Katahdin. The town is 14 miles south of Moosehead Lake, too, on the one paved road a visitor takes to reach that 118-square-mile miracle of rugged and preserved mountain water.

There are reasons for disbelief in a Monson future too. Twenty-five miles south and east of Monson — the preferred directions for economic vitality in Maine — Atkinson is weeks away from a vote to remove itself from the map, an action that will drop property taxes from $24 per $1,000 of home valuation to $6 per $1,000. Many there believe outsiders turned them into a land preserve, leaving only this choice.

The outsiders in Monson are bringing millions in investment that never existed in Atkinson, and an intention to bring Monson alive on the map. As Adkins is hearing it on the campaign trail, the plans are struggling to keep up with hard emotions. When you lose long enough, you see only more ways to lose. Adkins hears some positive responses about his push for broadband. He hears an echo, too, that digging in, and trusting only what you can see, is best.

The dean of the independent candidates in the Second, known and liked by both Tyler Adkins and Norm Higgins, is Kent Ackley. Ackley, 51, is from all the way down in Monmouth, a rural town in Lewiston's orbit. He had little business getting elected to the state Legislature when he ran against a Republican incumbent in 2016. Yes, he had an impressive boomerang resume

— graduating from local Monmouth Academy before heading off to Brown University. After he moved back, both he and his wife earned the credential of Maine Guide, experts in the outdoor Maine playground that attracts millions of visitors.

One of the first campaign news articles about Ackley back in 2016 noted that, when he was 18, he got in some big trouble in Monmouth. He and some friends stole an expensive computer from the high school. He spent a week in jail on a burglary conviction. He says now that people held him accountable for what he did as a stupid kid. They did not write him off for good. When he took out his nomination papers for Legislature in 2016, Ron Moody, the school principal when Kent stole that computer, was the first to sign. Ackley won with a 313-vote margin. The small town sorted it out.

The difference between the independents and the big leaguers on the congressional ticket is that the indies in places like the Second can still count on some measure of trust and individual connection. The indies are not more respectable than the big leaguers. It is just that they are playing a different game on a different field.

At the congressional level, the contest is about tribes and a duty to the ideological wins and losses that Higgins talks about. Congressional candidates are pressured to feed their tribes a diet — healthy or not — that gets them to 50.1 percent. Drifting off that path to nuance opens ways for an opponent to bludgeon you, rallying their tribe and confusing yours. Political operatives, donors, and candidates who want to win for duty to a larger purpose, or for personal glory, get conditioned not to be three-dimensional humans in a way that an Ackley, Adkins or Higgins can be.

Having won in the same year as Donald Trump, Ackley is skilled in divining the meaning of the president's victory in the Second. Why did this old place vote for Obama twice, by 12 percent and 8 percent, then turn to give Trump a 10-percent margin? Ackley has a Zen-like faith that it absolutely does not mean his rural neighbors are heading to a dark place.

"There's a ton of stuff about Trump that does not fit the values of rural Maine at all" and everyone, in his town, the county, and likely all the counties of the Second, knows it, Ackley says.

That just did not matter in 2016, he says, because the 2016 election was "a David and Goliath story." As implausible as it may seem to his friends in Portland and Boston, when Ackley goes door to door visiting with voters he hears people who see themselves as underdogs with moxie. David — the shepherd in the Bible story who is clever and, most critically, self-reliant, and who steps outside expectations and drops the giant with a single smooth stone. This is how the stoic voters of the Second see themselves. David is what they like to see in a candidate, Ackley says.

A trained economist, Ackley came home after running businesses in Rhode Island to run a tourism business in Monmouth. His neighbors are not nuts, he says. His neighbors are willing to risk an order that is not working for them. It is an order that does not speak to their self-concept of self-reliance or their everyday problems.

"Folks in rural Maine — and probably in rural America — are feeling left behind, left out and no one is really listening," Ackley says. "In 2008 and 2012, Obama seemed like David. In 2016, they looked at the two solutions that were presented to them and they said, "Okay, which one is David?" Trump seemed the most like David to them."

Ackley acknowledges that none of this can tell you a thing about which candidate is going to win the $31-million scrum for the Second's congressional seat this November. The candidates, Bruce Poliquin and Jared Golden, have lived as underdogs at times. They have found friends who are Goliaths too.

21

SOCIALIST

Before their first October debate the two congressional campaigns spend millions caricaturing each other and challenges such as poverty.

The tattoo ad goes after Golden for being in league with an amorphous "them" — people allegedly swimming in cash welfare. In truth, cash welfare is on a 22-year losing streak in the United States and in Maine. From 1996 forward, based on the new federal welfare reform policies, and the state rules that followed, the number of people getting temporary assistance for needy families shrank in Maine from 21,694 people with children in 1995 to 7,521 people with children in 2018.

Poliquin takes fire on health care. An ad in October shows Golden in a pub with Republican State Rep. Tom Saviello. The two drink a beer together to get across a message of bipartisan cooperation. Then, Saviello delivers a sound-bite blow: "I used to vote for Bruce Poliquin, but not after he voted to take away health care from 100,000 Mainers."

Poliquin's explanation around that soft spot is that he voted against repealing the Affordable Care Act before voting for repeals only when replacement protections were included. He has got some holes in that argument because the replacement language is general, not specific legislation trackable to outcomes for individuals.

There are bigger picture reasons for skepticism about the Affordable Care Act. Publicly funded health care in the form of Medicare and Medicaid is on a 50-year winning streak — more services, more lives covered, and most recently, the Affordable Care Act incentivizing states to expand health coverage through Medicaid and providing subsidies to people who do not have insurance through the workplace. With those investments, people still are not secure in their health care and the U.S. pays more for health care than other modern economies.

In a different world, maybe the attacks open a door to bigger conversation about health and welfare. This is not that world. This is the world of a multi-million congressional race that might tip the balance between Democratic and Republican control of the House. Both sides blunt and call all attacks false. They do not make the error of elaborating on their personal philosophy and saying what they might say privately about potential big changes. There is no room to look defensive with attempts to add facts or context.

Poliquin says none of his health care votes would have hurt anyone. He pivots to suspicion that the other guy is up to stuff that will threaten the voter's employer-based health insurance or their Medicare.

On the tattoo-takedown, the Golden campaign says federal rules prohibit any monkey business like welfare recipients buying tattoos or booze. Simple as that. They work the refs too. "No responsible media outlet should run that spot because it's bullshit," Bobby Reynolds says. The state newspapers report his comment as "bull (expletive)." The TV stations keep carrying the spot.

With this as the backdrop, expectations for a genteel first debate are low. Poliquin, whose Republican caucus colleagues have nicknamed the "energizer bunny," arrives perky. When Golden gets off a solid answer on a question about gun rights, it sparks the already-hyped incumbent into action.

"He referenced me so I'd like to respond," Poliquin says. "Jared is a young radical that embraces a socialist agenda. He cannot be trusted with our Second Amendment rights. He has a D rating with NRA (National Rifle Association). I have an A rating."

There is more rattling off about interest group ratings. Golden defends mechanically with examples of his work with gun owners in the Legislature.

The next topic, health care, repeats the pattern. Golden works his way to some momentum on the topic.

"I think there is no rational reason whatsoever why Congress has not given Medicare and Medicaid the authority to negotiate for lower drug prices. We allow the Department of Veterans Affairs to do that. That is also, I think, a very significant reform that Congress should be going after. Now, since I already know what's coming, I'm also going to go ahead and just say that we know what the record of Bruce Poliquin is in Congress. He voted to repeal the ACA (Affordable Care Act) without any plan to replace it whatsoever."

With that, Golden spells out the impact to the district, both in health insurance lost for individuals and extraction of Medicaid dollars from rural hospitals. Poliquin returns to his line of attack.

"Jared is a young radical that embraces a socialist agenda. He just throws stuff up on the TV and Nancy Pelosi's his biggest backer and so they put all these ads up on TV that are just not true."

At the next opportunity, Golden fires back on the socialist tag.

"We've been on TV all of 20 minutes, and the amount of lies coming out of Bruce's mouth are astounding. Twice, already, he's called me a socialist. I just want to address this, very clearly, for people. First of all, I served this country in Afghanistan and Iraq. Second, my first job in politics was working for a U.S. senator, Susan Collins, a Republican, on the Homeland Security Committee in the U.S. Senate. Lastly, through four years in the Maine state Legislature, I have worked across the aisle with Republicans on a number of very important bills and pieces of legislation, to help veterans, to protect youth from suicide, to make sure that we protect children from lead poisoning. Those bills would not become law if I was pushing some kind of socialist agenda. Now, let me tell you what's going on here, when Bruce says that, what he is suggesting is that I am somehow unAmerican. That is absolutely despicable."

When the moderator asks Poliquin if that is the suggestion, he responds:

"No, not at all. Jared Golden is the majority whip in the State House. That is a uniquely partisan job. Jared's job is to get all the Democrats together to vote in a pack. It's not to be bipartisan. Now, he mentions Susan Collins. Susan Collins supports me so I don't know why he keeps mentioning her. Here's another thing that's really important. Jared embraces a socialist agenda. That's his decision to do it. ..."

Golden attempts to interject with the moderator. "That's a lie ..."

Poliquin continues. "It's his decision to do it. Let me give you an example. Jared thinks it's a good idea to use welfare dollars to buy alcohol, tobacco, lottery tickets, and bail yourself out of jail. Here's another one. ... There's an organization in Maine called the Maine People's Alliance. Jared is a donor to the Maine People's Alliance, the most radical organization in Maine. They have endorsed him. He has welcomed that endorsement, and last week, it was the organization he donates to that bused people down to Washington to scream at Senator Collins, intimidate her. They are the same people who go out with bullhorns outside of our office. They didn't intimidate Senator Collins. They don't intimidate me. They're a socialist organization."

Golden pivots to his examples of Poliquin slipperiness.

"This is just an example of dirty politics," the challenger says. "Here's an example of how Bruce is misleading people. He says he supports access to health care. He voted to take it away from people. He says he supports better trade deals and things like tariffs, but the U.S. Chamber of Commerce is running ads thanking him for being anti-tariff. Bruce wants to be on both sides of every issue. You just can't trust him to be straightforward."

Before the debate starts, the moderator notes that Brett Kavanaugh has just been sworn in at the White House this day as an associate justice of the Supreme Court. The protests at Sen. Collins' office that come up in the debate tie to Collins' confirmation vote for Kavanaugh.

The Maine People's Alliance is another fault line. For forestry businesses, the People's Alliance is associated with environmentalism aligned with the legacy of the "Paper Plantation" report. In Lewiston, they have backed candidates for mayor who had come up short against Republicans. Democrats perceived as working class do well in Lewiston. Democrats perceived as having strong environmental or social welfare agendas fail. Incumbent Poliquin needs to push perception of Golden as a leftist to stunt the challenger's Lewiston vote. He is manic in the effort, which does not mean it will not work.

The major candidates call each other liars a few more times. The two independent candidates are pleasant and score no points. When the debate ends, Golden declines to shake Poliquin's hand. Pat Callaghan, moderator and journalist following Maine politics for 40 years, tweets later that the Poliquin-Golden animosity level is a new peak for Maine.

22

GUNS

Guns are a nerve center in figuring out how the Second might vote for Congress.

The New York Times visits in October. From the western mountains town of Phillips, their take on the race offers one quote from one voter. The man says: "I own a ton of guns."

Some efficient and not-so-subtle rural stereotyping there; every part of Maine, and America, has a hefty number of gun owners and guns. Still, the idea that the counties of the Second are more likely to reject gun regulation is correct. Guns matter here because they remind voters that they have a self-image of self-reliance and a heritage of hunting. Opposition to perceived gun regulation is magic dust for political strategists, a reliable reminder to voters of where they belong.

The Democratic Party side has "dog whistle" issues too, but nothing quite as reliable as the Republican side's opposition to gun regulation. Issues that can motivate a side to vote are the noisy spaces in campaigns; noise that is not about convincing people. Professionalized campaigns like the ones in the Second remind voters what they already think and stir those pots to motivate turnout at the polls.

Democrats hope Golden's Marine biography is a gun-issue neutralizer. His campaign runs a shooting range ad that never mentions gun regulation. The candidate announces that "while Bruce Poliquin hides from his votes to gut Social Security and Medicare, I'm a straight shooter." He then fires an obligatory round from a Remington rifle into the target's bullseye.

Poliquin keeps jabbing at gun rights in debates because anti-regulation sentiment is tangible. Two years earlier, every county in the Second rejected a referendum question that would have required background checks for the sale or transfer of a firearm between individuals. Right now, background checks apply to gun dealers in Maine. Regulating individual-to-individual transfer went down by nearly three-to-one in rural areas, including Golden's hometown of Leeds.

Public polling shows that Mainers are more open to gun regulation directed at irresponsible people. Golden's State House votes align with this outlook. When guns come up in a debate, he talks exclusively about legislative votes to allow courts to confiscate weapons from those charged with domestic violence. Outside the combat of debate he acknowledges a vote that went more directly against the agenda of gun rights organizations like the National Rifle Association and the Gun Owners of Maine — opposing the elimination of concealed carry permits that he sees "as an erosion of the background check system we have."

There are Golden positions that could irk backers of gun regulation. He opposes banning silencers. He stayed out of a protest some legislative colleagues joined against a sporting goods outlet selling assault-style weapons. "To me, that was just political grandstanding," Golden tells a newspaper columnist covering the campaign. "I'm not going to join some protest outside a business who is just following the law."

Risk that Golden's middle ground on guns will cost him votes on his left flank is eased by two factors — President Donald Trump and ranked choice voting. Passion for checking Trump is driving partisans to home base. Ranked choice voting is a kind of insurance policy for Golden too. The voter going for an independent candidate because of concern about gun violence still might give Golden a second-choice vote that could help him if the election is tight.

Immigration is a wedge issue playing loudly in other parts of the country. Poliquin takes care with it. In their second and final debate, he emphasizes his French-Canadian background and pivots to drugs "coming in from the Mexican border." In other places, Republican candidates are riffing about using their pickup trucks "to round up criminal illegals." Poliquin talks about "border security" and tries not to open doors to hot-button issues like separation of families at the border.

The heated attacks remain with health care — cross accusations about who will destroy Medicare — and guns.

On guns, Golden says, "What we need to do is keep a limited number of bad actors from getting their hands on any firearms, whatsoever, and, beyond that, we don't want to infringe on your Second Amendment rights whatsoever."

Poliquin rebuts with an attempt to disqualify Golden based on the ratings of gun interest groups. "I don't know how anybody with a 'D' rating from the NRA, an 'F' rating from the Gunowners of Maine, and (who) didn't even talk to the Sportsman's Alliance of Maine could ever even think about representing our Second District here in Maine."

The animosity is schoolyard, but real. Golden declines Poliquin's handshake again when the final debate ends.

23

ELECTION NIGHT

The candidate closing arguments take different turns.

In a sign that the Golden ad with state Sen. Tom Saviello is stinging, Poliquin sends out a mailer that says Golden is "a liar" for calling Saviello a Republican. The reality check is that Saviello is a maverick. He stomped on the toes of Democrats when he left their party in 2005 and won elections as a Republican five times.

Poliquin adds more partisan edge with a voter testimonial ad set at Simones in Lewiston. An older gentleman in a hot red U.S. Marine windbreaker and a doctor in a white coat theatrically state their truth that Golden is a radical. The congressman does not appear, and the ad, like the Congressman, never embraces President Trump directly. The spot is late-inning organ music pronouncing that the incumbent is one of "us." The production values are deliberately low. The energy is Trumpian.

Golden's team benefits from continuous airwave pounding on Poliquin around health care, mostly from the Democratic Congressional Campaign Committee and other outside groups. With the campaign's healthy budget, it has produced countless versions of its theme — Golden as Marine and middle-class everyman who will have your back. In the final week, they set most of the old versions aside and close with a new ad from Golden's wife endorsing her husband. A politician and child of central Maine's middle class in her own right, Isobel Moiles Golden is no prop. She speaks convincingly, restating the biography — Jared as "a son from a small business family" and "a Marine who signed up after 9/11."

"Most important for me," she concludes. "Jared has always put people first and he'll keep doing that in Congress."

For Democratic partisans and available independents, this is a pitch for optimism — give these kids a chance and they will have your back. For Trumpian partisans, it is another lefty scam.

On election morning, both candidates are showing obvious relief that the $31-million grind for the district is winding down. Poliquin, an energetic campaigner skilled in beelining to the friendliest zones of a high school football crowd, is shaking hands outside Rolly's Diner in Auburn.

"Everyone is glad that this thing is going to be over," he offers with a hoarse voice.

Just across the Androscoggin River in Lewiston, Golden stands with supporters waving campaign signs at commuters.

"It's out of my hands and it's in the hands of the voters and the field operation," he says, with relief identical to Poliquin's.

The challenger drives to Bangor to greet supporters there. On the way back, the water pump on his 2003 GMC Sierra pickup truck busts. The campaign finds him a lift to the Franco Center in Lewiston for their election eve gathering.

Poliquin is on his way to Dysart's near Bangor, a truck stop known for the best 5,000-calorie lumberjack meals in the state. When the votes start coming in, the news is obviously good for Democrats statewide and obviously undecided for Congress in the Second.

Janet Mills, the Democratic candidate for governor, gets the most votes ever for any gubernatorial candidate. It is a majority too — the first achieved by any candidate for governor in independent-minded Maine since Ken Curtis in 1970. A frequent sparring partner of LePage when she was state attorney general, Mills is now set to usher him off the stage in January and become the first woman to serve as Maine's governor.

Democrats grab commanding margins in the state Legislature too. First District U.S. Rep. Chellie Pingree, a Democrat, breezes to victory. Angus King, an independent U.S. senator who caucuses with Democrats and who incumbent Gov. LePage cannot stand, wins easily.

These wins are easier on the bigger Maine playing field that includes strong Democratic areas like Portland and coastal towns in York County. Golden is climbing slippery ledges and swatting black flies in the rural Second. Democrats are giddy to have a new governor and more legislators. With that, it is easier to miss the Democrat's sustained unpopularity in the rural pockets that is holding Golden back from a clear majority. An incumbent Democratic legislator loses his legislative seat in Somerset County's Pittsfield, a central Maine town, that gave Trump 54 percent, Clinton 33, and 13 percent to the Libertarians, the Greens and blank ballots combined. Tonight, the mix of motivated Democrats is helping Golden, just not massively. At 38 percent in Pittsfield, Golden is getting 5 percent more than Clinton two years earlier. Poliquin, at 52 percent, is just short of the Trump share there.

Mills wins handily for governor because she is a better retail politician than most understood. Fatigue with LePage and his governing hijinks that were "Trump before Trump" is factoring too. This is a good omen for Democrats everywhere that Trumpism could get rolled in two more years.

Still, the idea that Trump Republicanism got unquestionably crushed in Maine is not in the numbers. The independent candidates — a gauge of how surly Maine voters are with both parties — hold their own in places where they have just one major party opponent. State Rep. Kent Ackley, considered left-of-center moderate in rural Monmouth, gets re-elected against the same Republican he defeated in 2016. Yet, his margin shrinks so much that the race goes to recount, another sign that loyalty to Republicans in rural areas is steady. Norm Higgins, the Republican turned independent, wins in central Piscataquis County with 52 percent against a popular pediatrician who has run against him as a Democrat twice now and lost by the same 300-vote margin.

Personal politics matters in another rural pocket too. Although he loses, Tyler Adkins accomplishes something big that no one notices. He gets 40 percent of the vote in some of the most determined Trump country in the state and against a local incumbent, Paul Stearns, who all — including Adkins —

respect as a better man than Trump. The young man who boomeranged back from the Philippines wins his hometown of Monson too — even while Poliquin piles up a 60 percent margin against Golden there.

To the east, Atkinson moves ahead with its plan to vote itself out of existence with a hefty 187-to-19 margin. The news is of so little consequence that even the Bangor Daily News 30 miles to the east does not report it in their election coverage.

The night shows national Democrats on track to win more than 30 congressional seats and gain control of the House. The U.S. narrative focus is on young candidates seen as changing the party's old guard. In Queens, N.Y., Alexandria Ocasio-Cortez cruises to an expected general election victory after beating a likely future speaker of the House in the party primary. Ayanna Pressley, a Boston city councilwoman, becomes the first African American woman elected to Congress from Massachusetts. Ilhan Omar of Minneapolis becomes the first Somali-American elected to the U.S. House of Representatives. Democrats lose other potential milestone races by close margins — races for governor in Florida and Georgia and a U.S. Senate seat in Texas.

The Democratic triumph of the night — capturing the House — is built on close races and candidates like Golden, positioned as moderates. A fair number have military backgrounds too. Democrats put a dent in Trump. They acquire a vexing question for the next election — is it better to go with moderates like Golden or the passion of progressives? The numbers indicate that the moderates toiled through the harder terrain to win the House. The story lines, social media energy, and urban glitter are with the progressives.

Late on election night, the Maine campaigns of Golden and Poliquin anticipate what is next. When more rural town votes come in, the slim plurality enjoyed by Golden will shift to a slim plurality for incumbent Poliquin. No one is getting the required majority. Ranked choice voting lies ahead, potentially deciding a federal election for the first time in U.S. history. The 23,000 voters who chose independent candidates in the congressional race — if they made a second choice — are the deciders.

At the Franco Center, Golden is upbeat. Like Poliquin, he does not speak directly to ranked choice counting or court-battling likely to arrive with it. Another long game, with lawyers swapping in for ad-makers, is at hand.

"We've been here before. We were here in the primary," Golden tells supporters, trying to make the peculiar overtime ahead routine and predictable. "You all remember that night. We came down and we talked about how we had a lead and we were going to walk it forward from there to victory, so here we go."

Poliquin urges his crowd at Dysart's to go home and get some sleep.

"We're going to monitor this very closely," he says. "We're not going to get a final result tonight."

24

REFEREE

The campaigns know on election night that they are looking at weeks, not days, before this sport is settled.

A drawn-out calendar is how ranked choice tallying goes when a state does not have the tools to make it go fast. Plus, though neither campaign says it, both expect a legal fight will hitch onto the vote counting.

The referee for the count is Maine's Secretary of State Matt Dunlap, responsible for a tallying method so young that he cannot predict how many days it will take. The result will spring one congressional candidate to a 50-plus percent vote share and, with that, the Wonka golden ticket of incumbency in the U.S. House of Representatives, a status that lawyers for the other side will work to snatch away.

Dunlap is a man in the middle. Back in March, the secretary got under the skin of ranked choice voting supporters. He irritated them when he flagged a possible conflict — a reference to plurality voting in state statute books. The obstacle was enough to stop the printing of ranked choice ballots for June's primary, he said, and there may not be time to resolve it and get the new way in place.

This statement sprang a day or two of whispered speculation at the state capitol that the secretary, a Democrat, might be putting his thumb on the scale for Democratic gubernatorial candidate Janet Mills. The premise was that Mills stood a better chance against six primary opponents for governor without ranked choice voting. Before this notion of hanky-panky got any traction,

Dunlap and the attorney general's office backpedaled from his initial position. State courts took the question and, within weeks, ruled that recently adopted law allowing ranked choice held sway. Dunlap's office could go ahead and print ballots enabling voters to rank their choices for the June primary and, later, for the federal elections in November.

That little capitol snowball fight in March was nothing compared to what is now rolling toward Dunlap. Congressman Poliquin's election night statement that his campaign is "monitoring this very closely" is code that the tenacious incumbent is ready for a fight, as are the Democrats. Everyone needs something from Dunlap. Backers of ranked choice in Maine and nationally need Dunlap to execute a ranked choice count with flawless credibility, or the wheels of their reform might pop off. Democratic partisans need the same credibility to bolster their candidate, who stands the best chance of winning in a ranked choice count. Republicans need Dunlap to make mistakes, either political or legal, that could discredit the process.

Like it or not, Dunlap is now the proprietor of a ranked choice idea conceived by reformers and given political life — much as the reformers do not like to admit it — when Maine Democrats suffered brutal election losses to Gov. Paul LePage.

For the decade before LePage's election in 2010, ranked choice voting got introduced in most Maine state legislative sessions and died. Making it easier for independent candidates to compete with Democrats or Republicans was no easy starter with incumbent politicians. Spending at least several hundred thousand dollars to implement the idea — a process, not a bridge or a school — irked legislators too and gave them a reliable switchblade to kill ranked choice in legislative committees.

The path for ranked choice voting opened when "Trump-before-Trump" Republican LePage got elected. The circumstances of LePage's win lured Democrats — suspicious before of independent wonks trying to make politics "better" — to the idea of ranked choice voting.

The 2010 Maine governor's race essentially pitted two Democrats against LePage. Eliot Cutler, who as a legislative aide to Ed Muskie decades earlier had worked on the Clean Air and Clean Water acts, returned to Maine after a long career as a corporate lawyer. He was a founding partner of an environmental law firm that merged with the giant Akin Gump. He was running as an independent and reformer, threatening to the Democratic left as a corporate guy and inviting to middle-of-the-road Republicans looking for a way to give the state more credibility in commerce and avoid a future as Vermont with the Atlantic Ocean instead of Lake Champlain. The Democratic nominee was Libby Mitchell, beloved by party loyalists as speaker of the Maine House and proud traditional Democrat. LePage held down Tea Party Republicans and — in this phase before norm-busting Trump — made moderate Republicans nervous.

In the final week of that campaign, Democrats did something miraculous, a kind of self-imposed ranked choice when the rules still required just one choice. En masse, Democrats moved off their party's candidate and to the independent Cutler, a former Democrat. Voters do not normally behave like political strategists. Tens of thousands of Maine voters did exactly that in the campaign's final week. Polls showed Cutler, mired below 20 percent, flipping that position. Now, it was Democrat Mitchell sinking fast and Independent Cutler surging. The so-called "strategic voting" push that year became a painful, close-but-not-quite for Democrats. Cutler surged to within 10,000 votes of LePage and got 100,000 more votes than Democrat Mitchell. LePage won with 37.6 percent to 35.9 percent for Cutler.

Reformers do not like linking ranked choice to LePage's election because it frames what they believe is a good government reform for everyone in partisan terms. But, after 2010, ranked choice voting gathered obvious momentum. It finally got a legislative vote, losing in 2013. With fuel from LePage winning another plurality victory in 2014, ranked choice reformers were able to go around reluctant legislators and gather enough signatures for a voter referendum. In November 2016, Maine voters approved ranked choice with a 52 percent margin. Legal interpretations around the state Constitution would limit ranked choice to primaries for statewide offices and federal general elections for Congress.

Secretary of State Dunlap, with scars from dustups around ranked choice going back years, is the new way's chief implementer. He stands an excellent chance, too, of traffic-copping a ranked choice rarity — a count that flips the order of plurality finishers. Any party wronged — by their definition, not winning — has incentive, lawyers, and dollars — to discredit Dunlap.

With that, battling Dunlap is harder than it looks. He grew up in Bar Harbor and settled in Old Town after running track a long time ago at University of Maine. At 5-foot-6, with sturdy glasses and a compact build, he looks better suited for tunneling than running. Bartender and fur trapper were among his odd jobs before he ran for the state Legislature. He told funny stories. Did his job. People liked him. The voters in Old Town, an old logging town recently battered by the closure of a paper mill, elected him as a Democratic state representative four times, with margins that left him unopposed in his last race. Democratic colleagues in the Legislature then chose him five times for secretary of state. His one electoral loss was a long-shot bid to get the party's nomination for U.S. Senate in 2012.

Dunlap is a type underestimated by flatlanders — a son of the Second who stays home. His caginess shows early in the Trump administration when he joins an eclectic mix of characters appointed to the Presidential Commission on Election Integrity. Democrats view the commission, chaired by Kansas' Republican Secretary of State Kris Kobach, as a kangaroo court for presidential paranoia and base-voter excitement-making. The group starts with weak credibility, and efficiently earns none. The White House makes the appointments. A Democrat of lesser ego, Dunlap is a fig leaf for Republicans to claim bipartisanship and a monitor, at least, for Democrats. His role is to poke his head into a henhouse full of preening foxes and limit harm.

Without naiveté, and likely with coordination with national Democrats who see the commission as a dangerous chew toy for xenophobic Republicans, Dunlap takes a path from charmer to aggressive plaintiff. Vice President Mike Pence emcees the first meeting of the "bipartisan" commission at the White House in the summer of 2017. With the room structured like a congressional hearing, Pence recognizes Secretary Dunlap of Maine for five minutes. Dunlap deadpans that he did not have any prepared remarks but "would keep it within the 45-minute allotment." Always solid in his comedic timing, Dunlap gets warm laughter in a stiff room. He speaks for three minutes. He folksily explains that a typical election problem in Maine is an absentee ballot forgotten "in a pile of seed catalogs." The commission's work should strive to instill confidence, he says, "in an electoral process that belongs to the American people."

Less than three months later, Dunlap sues the commission. He alleges bias in the makeup of the commission and withholding of agendas, schedules, and information from him and other participants. A federal District Court judge sides with Dunlap. Early in 2018, the White House dissolves the commission citing lawsuits.

Dunlap's legal challenge got built on the technical requirements of something called the Federal Advisory Committee Act. But, in local media discussions about his lawsuit, Dunlap always makes sure to drop in a memorable example of information not shared. He and other commission members, Dunlap says, were not told when a commission staffer got arrested for possessing child pornography. Commissioners were blindsided by news reporters about this troubling development, Dunlap says. Surely, he says, routine information sharing around such matters is important.

Dunlap never mentions — and only the most naïve would find it coincidental — that the staffer busted with the pornographic images got hired from the ranks of activist Republicans with prebaked views and answers around alleged election fraud. Dunlap is mainly the humble public servant he presents himself to be, but — in the spirit of the Second — if you screw with him or with elections, he is capable of and comfortable screwing you right back.

25

COUNTING ROOM

Unofficial returns from all cities and towns the day after the election show the new starting line — Bruce Poliquin: 134,184 votes; Jared Golden: 132,013; independent Tiffany Bond: 16,552; independent William Hoar: 6,875.

As expected, neither top candidate is close to the 50 percent required to win. Incumbent Poliquin stuck at 46.2 percent of the vote; Golden stuck at 45.5 percent.

The two independent candidates, Bond and Hoar, declare during the race that Golden is their second choice. Team Golden feels good about their opportunity to rake in enough ranked choice votes to win. The chase for the Second is ending where it began. Poliquin is ahead, and with the power of incumbency. Golden owns potential.

The candidates drop from sight. The Goldens are inside their Lewiston neighborhood home running through a Netflix watchlist backlog. Congressman Poliquin is letting the Maine Republican Party do most of the talking. The grind now is with Secretary of State Dunlap and his band of ballot-processing civil servants.

Ranked choice voting operates with mundane math. The first look is to the ballots of the last-place finisher — William Hoar with those 6,875 votes. If his voter made a second choice of Poliquin or Golden, that one gets his vote. If he made no second choice, nothing happens.

Because the small number of votes for Hoar is not enough to push either candidate to a majority, the process is going to repeat with the 16,552 votes for Tiffany Bond. The new tally will leave Poliquin or Golden above 50 percent, the second-place finisher below 50 percent and Bond and Hoar at zero percent because their votes are reassigned or, if no other ranked choices were made, off the table.

This process could be an "instant" runoff if all those voter choices lived on one hard drive. They do not. Maine has 500 local voting jurisdictions — cities, towns, and unorganized territories. Many of these places count votes in the quintessential New England way — by hand. The ballot boxes are sealed and kept locally. Results of these local counts are reported to the secretary of state's office.

Ranked choice is a different animal. Counters need data about choices from every ballot. Making this happen requires shipping hundreds of ballot boxes to Augusta, the state capital. In a bowling alley of a room with baby-blue walls, Dunlap's staffers are unsealing those boxes and electronically scanning ballots, so all voter choices are in one place.

This runs like an election recount. Lawyers and staffers for the campaigns are feet away behind loops of plastic chain purchased at a discount store. They watch the monotony of scanning ballots on a single jumbo machine, checking details like the match between the number of ballots reported on election night locally and the number scanned.

There are two opposing stories about what this scene of clattering steel ballot boxes, a humming scanner, and gaggling campaign lawyers represents.

Democrats see democracy in action — a new and better way to achieve a majority winner. Louisiana and Georgia are among states that require a majority winner. When no one gets a majority in those states, the top two would run-off in a new election a month or so later. To Maine Democrats and ranked choice voting advocates, this is the sight and sound of an instant runoff, avoiding all the fuss of a second election and giving Maine a majority winner for Congress.

Republicans see sleight of hand. They brew the new, ballot-scanning activity with suspicion of modern technology. "No one is able to review the algorithm used by the computer to determine elections," a Poliquin campaign spokesperson offers. "The artificial intelligence is not transparent."

When all the votes get pulled in, it will be possible to go to a state website and download 300,000 spreadsheet rows showing the choices and non-choices made on every ballot cast. In that sense, the Poliquin statement is wrong. This process is tedious, not mystical. Still, when it comes to how people think — and potential to sow mistrust — team Poliquin has something to work with. The process is transparent only for math nerds or activists paid to learn this stuff.

In the cramped counting room, Dunlap — a state constitutional officer elected by the Legislature — visits to field media questions, mostly about when his staff expects to complete the work. Julie Flynn — a civil servant and deputy secretary of state — runs the counting room. One wag, a former State House news reporter, likens Flynn to Maine's Mount Katahdin — a quiet and immovable force of civil process. In approving ranked choice voting twice, Maine voters had handed civil servants like Flynn sticky yarn. In a perfect world, each of the 500 voting jurisdictions in Maine would own equipment to scan ballots. All the voter choice data then could get securely and instantly transited for a central ranked choice tally.

Maine enjoys worry-free election security. The state never went down the road of electronic voting systems. No one is making noises that the Russians may have hacked in. At the same time, the state's traditional, localized election process is not built to put the "instant" in this runoff. Larger Maine cities and towns have mechanical counters to tally their paper ballots and provide a memory stick with the data. The many small towns do not have those tools, but they have a modest enough number of ballots that traditional elections run smoothly. By 11 p.m. on election nights about 90 percent of precincts have reported. In all but the most razor-thin races, elections are done on election night and every step has paper ballot backup. The profile of Maine elections — hyperlocal voting service, short lines, and high trust — is bedrock. That strength does not translate easily to an innovation like ranked choice voting, so the job falls to counters and checkers like Flynn.

Flynn's team does catch one break. They got the chance to live-test their fatiguing process back in June with two elections that were not so tight. In the Democratic primary for Congress, Golden had beaten Lucas St. Clair 46 percent to 38 percent in the traditional count. When ranked choice added the preferences of voters who selected other candidates, Golden won 54 to 46-percent. Similarly, the Democratic candidate for governor, Janet Mills, won a traditional plurality of 33 percent in a seven-candidate field. Through multiple rounds of assigning choices from voters whose candidates were not in the top two, Mills won 54 to 46 percent.

The counting room during June's preamble was a cocktail party compared to the anxiety now. Back then, only one party — Democrats who are more favorable to ranked choice — were involved. The traditional returns pointed to leading candidates ultimately winning anyway. There were no lawsuit threats.

Those June races made it more difficult to fire suspicion about ranked choice voting. State media got an up-close look at the duo of Dunlap and Flynn. Dunlap, the pol, telling stories and slapping backs. Flynn, the technical expert beyond reproach, who — typical of the culture in Maine's unorganized territories where she grew up — might look exhausted but would never stop. Media and campaigns saw that ranked choice meant extra work. No one close to the scene suspected the people doing the work. November, with its higher-dollar race and potential to flip the order of finish, tests whether this center of trust will hold.

The first volleys are aimed at Dunlap. A few days into the counting, on Veterans Day weekend, the Maine Republican Party posts on Facebook that some of the ballot boxes being transported to Augusta have no locks. They allege bias in Dunlap's team too. One of the workers scanning ballots, they say, has made favorable posts on social media about candidate Golden. They beg relief. The man should be reassigned.

State workers have the Monday after Veterans Day off, except for Dunlap's ballot scanners who are still receiving ballot boxes from towns. They expect they need two more days to get all choices in one place, then they will push a laptop button to riffle through the data and declare a winner.

Dunlap gets a request in the counting room to respond to the Republican Party's questions about security and bias. He gathers what passes for a press gaggle in Maine — one television camera, an Associated Press reporter, and a couple of interested bystanders — in a hallway. He bats away the concern about locks first. The requirement is a seal that must be cut away he says. No boxes have shown up from the towns without seals, he says, and the vast majority have locks too. He has no concern about ballot tampering.

He got folksy and sarcastic when asked about the alleged staffer bias.

"We've had a talk with Andy and we've told him that if he's going to like Jared's tweets (he) probably should like Bruce's too, because we don't want anyone's feelings to get hurt," Dunlap says. "Look, this is politics and I understand that it's all about platforming and positioning, but I don't ask people's political affiliations when I hire them."

A better course for sharing serious concerns, Dunlap suggests, would be calling him or walking up to him in the counting room where Republicans have representatives, not posting on Mark Zuckerberg's app.

Dunlap wins the media round. Nonpartisans — exhausted by both campaigns' tsunami of ads — are not signaling suspicion about the ranked choice overtime. Dunlap keeps inviting the public to the counting room to see what is happening for themselves. Only campaign operatives and lawyers appear.

The next day, Josh Tardy, a lawyer and a former Republican state legislative leader, is chatting with Dunlap in the back of the counting room. He mentions that the lawyer from Washington, D.C., that Republicans have hired to sue Maine is a Dunlap lookalike. It is true. Lee Goodman, a former Federal Elections Commission chairman appointed by President Barack Obama, has a bald head and prominent glasses, just like Dunlap.

Maybe Tardy is just making small talk. Maybe he is trying to get in Dunlap's head or get the secretary to say something clever that could pop into a legal brief. Dunlap says "no kidding" about the doppelganger thing. He changes the topic to hunting.

One day later, Goodman files suit in federal District Court in Bangor on behalf of Poliquin and Second District voters. In Brett Baber, et al. versus Matthew Dunlap, et al., he seeks a restraining order to stop the tallying. The ranked choice tabulation might never happen.

26

WINNER

Congressman Poliquin assembles a noon-hour press conference at the state capitol shortly after his lawsuit is filed.

His prepared remarks avoid detailed legal argument. On this day after Veterans Day, he honors the 1.5 million men and women who died throughout the nation's history defending freedom and "the rule of law that is detailed in the United States Constitution, including our voting rights."

Poliquin whacks at the shins of ranked choice — "a circus" using "a black-box, computer algorithm." His message discipline is dogged, always calling the new voting law "rank choice," never "ranked choice" voting.

"We already know that the engineered, rank choice, vote-counting system is illegal under the Maine Constitution," Poliquin says. "It's now time to find out if the rank voting system is illegal under the U.S. Constitution."

In this, he refers to state court rulings that narrowed the use of ranked choice voting to party primaries and federal offices because the state constitution has a reference to plurality voting.

The questioners, familiar with the rarity of Poliquin pressers, try to knock the congressman off his planned course. They get nothing new.

Would he concede if the judge ruled against him? Poliquin does not say he would; he does not say he would not; he gets by with it. One reporter gets testy with Poliquin for not telling "the whole story" about what the state court decision means. Poliquin ignores him. Reporters can add the context that state courts allowed the new voting method to go forward, if they like. He is not going to acknowledge anything that does not fit with making ranked choice voting look suspect.

Back at that counting room, Dunlap volleys off a request from the Maine Republican Party to cease his work until the court rules on the restraining order. When a judge speaks, Dunlap says, he will follow. Until then, the work pushes on. He estimates they likely need only one more day.

The next day brings a cascade of bad news for the Poliquin campaign. Federal Judge Lance Walker in Bangor rejects Poliquin's request for an immediate order to stop the ranked choice tally. He schedules a full hearing on the lawsuit for Dec. 5. That same morning, Dunlap informs the campaigns and state media outlets that his team is done with the hard part: loading all the voter choices into one system. At noon, they will tally the data and announce the winner.

This sets the table for a strange and adorable scene of civic performance art. The secretary of state's team sets up a portable screen — the type most commonly found in middle schools during the 1980s — in their counting room. Dunlap and Julie Flynn preside. The idea is to project the data crunching live — in full view of the public and the campaigns.

Television cameras jam forward to the demarcation line of plastic chain. Reporters are where they have been all week — seven feet from the counters. Only, this time, the counters promise news — a milestone, a possible end to the chase for the Second. Each mundane step projects from a nearby laptop to the screen. Campaign lawyers and reporters watch Microsoft Windows open. They see some Excel spreadsheets open. They listen to each click here, each scroll. This scintillating action drifts on for 10 minutes, experienced as an hour. Dunlap tries play by play to liven the office work. This fails. The event is akin to forcing the Kentucky Derby gallery to watch accountants instead of horses.

At last, the process circles to a place where Dunlap feels safe dropping a line he may have practiced in the mirror this morning: "Who won the election?"

There is delay — seconds that seem like minutes. Another Excel spreadsheet opens. This one has fewer numbers. It has some black numbers, some blue numbers, some red numbers. Everyone is at their eye doctor now, squinting. Which line am I supposed to read? With some pointing from Dunlap and Flynn, the news comes into view:

Jared Golden now has 50.53 percent of the vote; Congressman Bruce Poliquin has 49.47 percent. The choices from voters who did not make these men their first choice have added 10,232 votes to Golden and 4,695 votes to Poliquin. Golden now has 139,231 votes; Poliquin has 136,326. Pending court action, Golden wins. At age 36, he is the likely new U.S. representative for one of the oldest congressional districts in the nation, Maine's quirky, vast and proud Second. He is the first Democrat to defeat an incumbent Republican here, and his dad is proved correct in what he said in October about his son's endeavor: Jared is serious about it.

There is almost nothing in the way of hoots or hollers when the election results pop on the screen. Jon Breed, Golden's campaign manager, squeezes into the room just before the result show. He walks out immediately after the data display, just as stone-faced as when he walked in. There is more work ahead — a press conference for candidate Golden to push the perspective that the young Marine is now the inevitable congressman.

Within an hour, the same press corps that witnessed the secretary of state's audio-visual club meeting gathers at the state capitol to hear from Golden. Golden bolsters the credibility of ranked choice voting with care, trying not to look self-serving. He uses the full runoff election process in play in other states as a straw man.

"Who in this state wants to see another campaign commercial wedged between Thanksgiving and Christmas?" he asks. "I don't think anyone. So, I think that this was a good system and it has worked well."

Golden thanks entrants to the race for stepping into the public arena, without mentioning the incumbent congressman or independent candidates by name. He takes heat out of the conflict when asked if he has anything to say about Poliquin's pledge to continue his legal appeal.

"That's his decision to make," Golden says. "I respect that."

This is the Golden campaign's best day. But, with a Dec. 5 federal court date on the calendar, there are no public victory laps. A few staffers smatter applause when the congressman-elect finishes his remarks. They are not riding a wave. They are climbing a muddy hill, still.

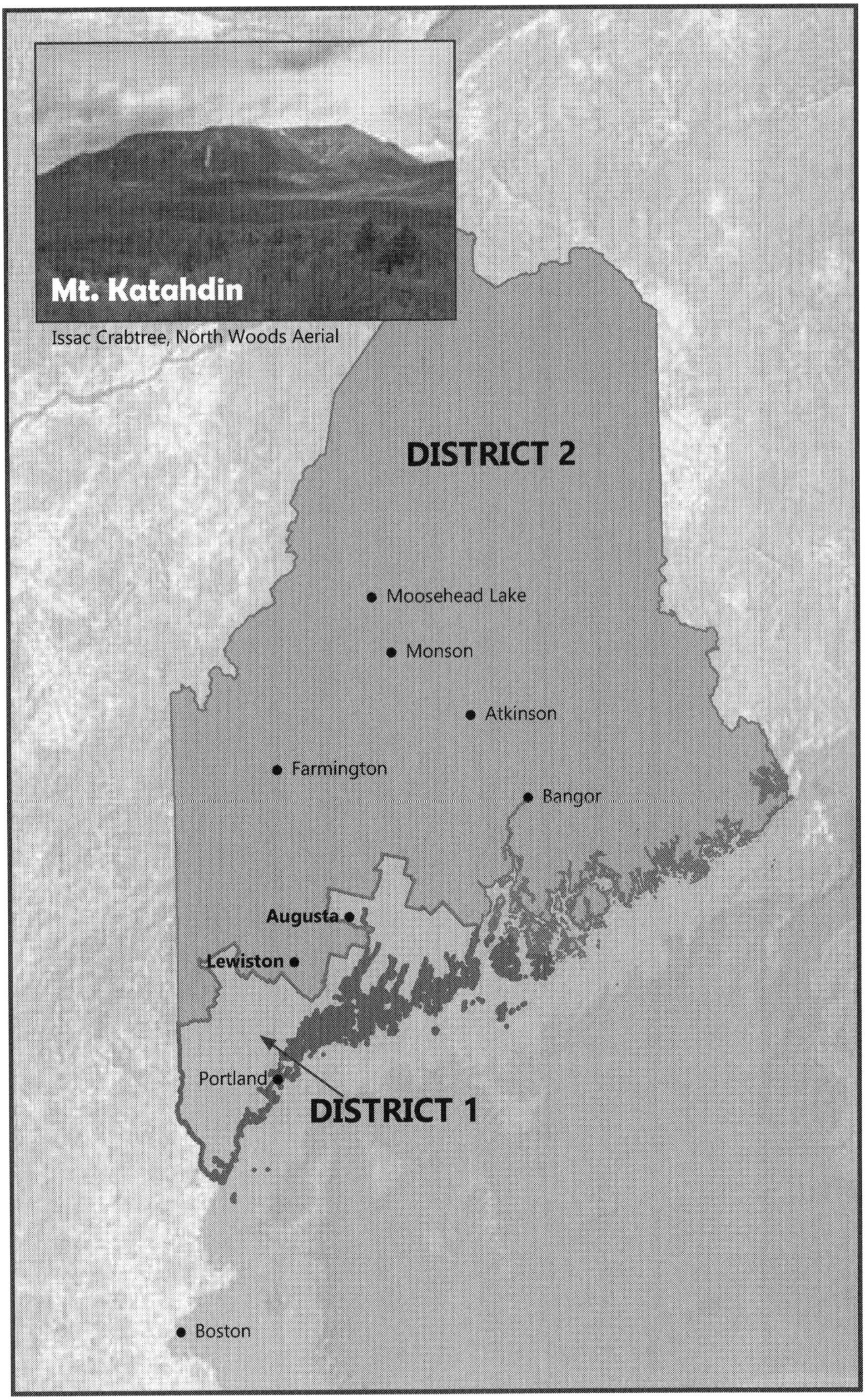

Mt. Katahdin
Issac Crabtree, North Woods Aerial

DISTRICT 2

● Moosehead Lake

● Monson

● Atkinson

● Farmington

● Bangor

Augusta ●

Lewiston ●

Portland ●

DISTRICT 1

● Boston

Lewiston

Daniel J. Marquis Photography

Monson

Issac Crabtree, North Woods Aerial

Moosehead Lake

Issac Crabtree, North Woods Aerial

The Campaign Trail

Jared Golden at Bates College, 2009, and at Campaign Press Conference Nov. 2018

Photo Left: Jose Leiva, Lewiston Sun Journal. Photo right: Joe Phelan, Kennebec Journal

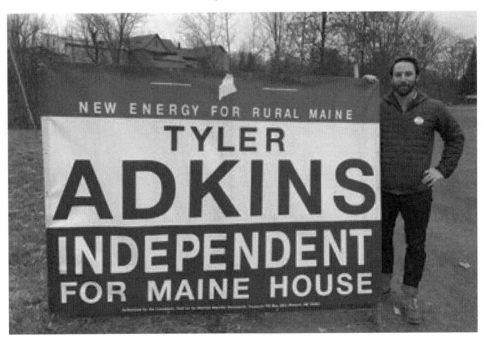

Tyler Atkins, Monson Maine, Election Day 2018.

Bruce Poliquin and son Sam, winning primary election for Congress, 2014

Photo: Carl D. Walsh, Portland Press Herald

Julie Flynn and Matt Dunlap of Secretary of State's office manage ranked choice voting count, Nov. 2018

Photo: Joe Phelan, Kennebec Journal

27

COURTHOUSE

> "Man's curiosity, his relentlessness, his inventiveness, his ingenuity have led him into deep trouble. We can only hope that these same traits will enable him to claw his way out."
> **E.B. White**, a letter from Brooklin, Maine

Those campaign donations are now funding an exodus of campaign lawyers from their traditional homeland in Washington, D.C., to U.S. District Court in Bangor, Maine.

The attorneys find 50 students from Hermon High School filling the federal courtroom when they arrive Dec. 5 for a 9 a.m. election dispute hearing. Jesse Hargrove, the educator who guided the teens onto a bus earlier, is pumped. A teacher for 17 years, Hargrove is always on the prowl for ways to engage students in civic life and the law. A couple of years back, he and the Hermon High team got the state Supreme Court to hold an oral argument at the high school. When he contacts federal court officials in nearby Bangor about attending the election hearing they are welcoming and offer room for 50. This means every junior or senior in the small high school with an interest is in the room.

On the bench, U.S. District Court Judge Lance Walker is a child of the Second too. His dad was an engineer on the Canadian Pacific Railway. Later, his mom and dad ran a store and travel agency in Dover-Foxcroft, the largest town in Piscataquis County with 4,000 people now. Walker made a journey typical for youth from the Second — from the high school in Dover-Foxcroft to the University of Maine in Orono, still within the boundaries of the vast rim counties, and then to the University of Maine Law School in Portland. He stayed in the nerve center of Maine's economy, becoming a partner at the well-respected Portland law firm of Norman, Hanson and DeTroy.

his election case drops on Walker's docket just weeks into his tenure as a federal district judge. His formal installation — called a robing ceremony — is still in the works. Ahead of that, the 46-year-old elevated from the state courts will host an election fracas at a moment of peak cynicism around politics and the federal courts. Seven weeks earlier, the disputed nomination of Brett Kavanaugh to the U.S. Supreme Court clears the U.S. Senate on a 50-48 vote. Sen. Susan Collins' vote to confirm stokes partisanship in Maine. The view that federal courts are just one more mosh pit for politics lives strong in the Twitter-sphere and cable news shows hunting for their 500,000 viewers in the critical age 25 to 54 demographic.

Walker's professional biography should offer powerful potential for paranoia among Maine Democrats. Their nemesis, Gov. Paul LePage, first appointed Walker to the Maine District Court in 2014. Sixteen months later, LePage elevated Walker to an opening on the state's Superior Court. Then, earlier in 2018, President Donald Trump nominated Walker for the federal District Court.

The names LePage and Trump push the buttons of Maine Democrats. And yet, in Bangor, the only noticeable mob anywhere near the courthouse is exceeding polite — Hargrove's charges from the justice and law classes at Hermon High School.

The same holds true in the counting room, the press conferences, and all public events associated with this toss-up election. With the presidential election case of Bush v. Gore in the Democrats' library of pain, it should be easy to stir their fear. Instead, when prodded, Maine Democrats project genuine confidence in their case and the judge. One ranked choice advocate with long experience in Maine politics shrugs off the matter of who appointed Judge Walker. He respects the firm where Walker had practiced. That is good enough for him. The so-called norms of civic behavior that national commenters fret about are doing more than holding in the Second. Faith in the institution to sort stuff out in Bangor is slate-hard, heatproof.

Walker takes command of the unusual hearing. The initial arguments are about what testimony should be allowed. In addition to the principals —

116

dendant Secretary of State Dunlap, represented by the state attorney general's office; Poliquin's lawyer, Lee Goodman from the Washington, D.C., firm of Wiley Rein — there are lawyers for independent candidate Tiffany Bond and ranked-voting advocates.

Poliquin's team amended their initial complaint after Walker denied their injunction request. They want the judge to either invalidate the ranked choice count and install the traditional count as the election's result or to order a new election with just the two top candidates. Either course is a difficult get. Third parties, such as Bond's attorney, are there to make the argument that their voters had gone to the polls and made their choices with full understanding of the rules. Changes now, their practical argument goes, are changing the rules in the middle of the game.

The Poliquin argument takes many tacks. His team argues that Article I of the U.S. Constitution requires a plurality standard in elections. They make a due process claim, built on the idea that some voters could not comprehend ranked choice well enough to cast a meaningful vote. They make a First Amendment claim, based on the election law giving more voice to some voters than others. They allege violation of the Voting Rights Act.

The first order of business is whether the Poliquin side is going to be allowed to bring forward an expert in voter behavior, political science Professor James Gimpel from the University of Maryland. Gimpel sits among the high school students as lawyers argue about whether his testimony is appropriate.

Walker allows Gimpel to testify. This does not help. Gimpel acknowledges that while he has questions about how certain voters were responding to the ranked choice system, he has not talked with any Maine voters. On the law and the facts, the hearing is a good day for lawyers on the side of Golden and ranked choice voting. The only person happier than these lawyers is teacher Hargrove.

"This hearing was perfect for my students," he says afterward. "It had elements that were like a trial, with lawyers objecting and making arguments, and other parts that were like an oral argument before an appellant court."

CHASING MAINE'S SECOND

The new U.S Congress is getting sworn in four weeks. Walker tells the courtroom that he will rule soon on whether challenger Golden or incumbent Poliquin have the law on their side in representing the Second.

28

END OF THE ROAD

One week after the hearing, Judge Walker brings his gavel down on plaintiff Poliquin. The result is not surprising. The thoroughness is stark.

Walker sees team Poliquin connecting no dots in their constitutional arguments. Their Article 1 angle is 180 degrees off. Far from wanting to dictate how states conduct elections, Walker says, the framers of the Constitution sought decentralization.

"It is clear from The Federalist Papers and other public debates leading up to the ratification of the Constitution that federalism was its intellectual lodestar and was to act as a bulwark against the perceived threat of centralized political authority by allowing for political tolerance," he writes.

The insistence in critiquing ranked choice voting, paired with pleas for judicial intervention, irritate Walker.

"A majority of Maine voters have rejected that criticism and Article 1 does not empower this Court to second guess the considered judgment of the polity on the basis of the tautological observation that ranked choice voting may suffer from problems, as all voting systems do," the judge writes.

Poliquin — persistent to the end — appeals to the First Circuit Court of Appeals in Boston. On Dec. 21, the First Circuit denies Poliquin's appeal of Walker's decision with a one sentence notation that the congressman does not "have a strong likelihood of success on the merits."

Poliquin closes the book on the election with a concession via Twitter on the day before Christmas. "Despite winning the largest number of votes on

Election Day, I believe it's in the best interest of my constituents and all Maine citizens to close this confusing and unfair chapter of voting history by ending any further legal proceedings," Poliquin writes. "Although we may disagree on the issues, I wish Jared Golden personally the best during the coming term."

An election formality brings some drama. On Dec. 28, Gov. Paul LePage signs a certificate generated from the secretary of state's office that officially certifies Golden's election to Congress. LePage tweets a picture of the certificate. Next to his initials he adds the words, "Stolen Election."

"Ranked Choice Voting didn't result in a true majority as promised — simply a plurality measured differently," LePage tweets with the inscribed certificate. "It didn't keep big money out of politics & didn't result in a more civil election."

Asked to respond, Golden uses LePage as a foil to make a play for more voters who do not like squabbling.

"Maine people are tired of this kind of poor leadership, which is why they voted for change in November," he says.

The holiday timing precludes any victory lap for Golden. As always, he is cautious too. The first Democrat ever to beat an incumbent Republican in the Second has the tight, ranked choice win to thank, both for getting him across the line and for disguising his accomplishment.

The Second — a frontier bigger, brawnier and more interesting than the rest of New England in so many ways — now joins New England in completing a political divide. All 21 U.S. House districts across Connecticut, Rhode Island, Massachusetts, New Hampshire, Vermont, and, now, Maine are held by Democrats.

29

OUT OF THE WOODS

"Some people are still unaware that reality contains
unparalleled beauties. The fantastic and unexpected, the
ever-changing and renewing is nowhere so exemplified as
in real life itself." **Berenice Abbott**, photographer

The Second's new congressman arrives at a U.S. Capitol buzzing about progressive Democrats. U.S. Rep. Alexandria Ocasio-Cortez from Queens, N.Y., has 3.8 million Twitter followers. U.S. Rep. Jared Golden from Lewiston brings his mere 4,000 tweeters. He keeps a campaign commitment not to support Nancy Pelosi, California Democrat, for speaker of the House. The speaker likely welcomes one less vote in exchange for a more reliable hold of all New England.

***

The Maine Legislature crushes a couple of bills to end ranked choice voting. Democrats propose a state constitutional amendment to extend ranked choice voting to general elections for governor and the Legislature. Their amendment needs a two-thirds majority and comes up short with 60 percent; Democrats mostly supportive and Republicans mostly opposed. Then, in the fall, Democrats get support from Gov. Janet Mills to initiate ranked choice voting in the federal election for president in 2020. The electoral votes for Maine — two assigned based on the statewide result and one for the results in each congressional district — will get tallied using ranked choice voting.

"Ranked choice voting for president in Maine is an historic first," declares FairVote president and CEO Rob Ritchie. "Swing states like Maine effectively decide the presidency, and the White House should not be decided by a 'spoiler.'"

California, New York, Minnesota, and Massachusetts are enabling rank choice voting in more local elections. So far, Maine is the one state opening the door on federal elections. FairVote tries to entice Republican support with scenarios of how votes for Libertarian candidates could swing to Republicans in a ranked choice system. So far, few Republicans are buying.

***

Maine chooses Joe Hennessey of Piscataquis Community High School as its Teacher of the Year for 2019. This honor, for him and Piscataquis County, is a platform and, when asked, he raises awareness about social barriers limiting student potential. Educators across the state need support getting students to school every day, he says, and removing barriers to learning, especially unrecognized trauma and basics like nutritious meals.

***

The town of Atkinson is underway with eliminating itself. The county will take control of road maintenance in July. The town hall will go on the market. There is no loss of a local school because children were bused before. Property taxes paid by all unorganized territories are enough to fund schools. The new wrinkle is that the state manages transportation, assignment of schools, and alternatives. There is loss of local control, but no drop off in school quality.

***

The Maine Legislature re-elects Matt Dunlap as secretary of state. Julie Flynn, his deputy, testifies in February on a bill to require voters to present identification at the polls. Flynn tells lawmakers the proposed law is a "solution for which there is no documented problem." The bill dies in committee on a largely party-line vote.

***

Former Rep. Bruce Poliquin makes noises through the winter that he may compete for Congress again. On Facebook, he's talking about immigration with a more Trumpian edge and backing the stretcher that Special Counsel Robert Mueller's report to the Justice Department is proof of nothing more to see. His economic emphasis remains low taxes and deregulation as the path to revitalize the Second.

Come summer, the former congressman steps back. He announces on Facebook that caring for his aging parents will make any run in 2020 impossible. Then adds: "I'm itching to run again to right the rank voting scam which gave my win — our win — on Election Day to the candidate who came in second place. I'm eager to help our president secure our borders and stop the invasion of illegal aliens . . ."

"There are lots of ways I'm already helping Republicans win next November. Then we'll see what the future holds for 2022. . . . We're not done yet!"

If President Trump were to lose in 2020, the Poliquin political career put on track with good timing in 2014 stands a better chance of a comeback with fresh good timing in 2022. Right now, opponents are tagging the former congressman a sore loser, and yet, he stays on the path of all successful politicians, he persists. In September, President Trump appoints Poliquin to a volunteer position, chairing the board of the Securities Investor Protection Corporation. The board oversees professional staff engaged in recovering assets for investors when brokerage houses, such as Lehman Brothers, fail.

U.S. Rep. Golden is steering a course of political reform and health care commitment. In the wake of a government shutdown, he sponsors a bill with Texas Republican Dan Crenshaw, also a veteran, to deny salaries to Congress during any government shutdown. Five months later, the bill has not moved out of committee.

On economics, Golden's most central position is defense of federal funding streams for health care flowing to the Second, which — more than most constituents understand — are holding local economies together.

***

Daniel Bailey, owner of Zimmie's Comics in Lewiston, gets an offer in the spring that would be reckless to turn down. The owners of DotCom Comics and Collectibles offer to buy all of Bailey's inventory if he will operate a new store of theirs closer to Portland.

This offer, flattering and valuable, is not something Bailey can automatically accept. He needs to ask his customers. If his community says stay, Bailey will stay. In Bailey's determined and quintessentially northern and eastern Maine view of things, this is just how it is. In unison, the customers who are also his friends and his community, say he should take the offer and go. They are subscribers to the same rule book, looking out for Bailey just as he is looking out for them. His loyal customers will get on the interstate and make their visits to the new store. That is just the way it is.

Later that spring, Lewiston has another empty storefront to fill. Freeport, just north of Portland and home to the global L.L. Bean brand, gains another amenity in the new DotCom Comics and Collectibles store operated by Bailey. His suggestions on merchandise are driving sales. He is another talent of the Second — expert in comics, superheroes, and games — exported. The cloud of financial worry that surrounded Bailey in the fall is gone. He is happy.

***

Winter at the closed Monson Elementary School is quiet. On the walls are photographic portraits worthy of metropolitan museums. Restored from glass plates by artist and photographer Todd Watts, the images of North Woods life 100 years ago reboot the viewer. There is a baseball team, half in wool uniforms and half in street clothes; a quarryman perched with pulleys. Black and white, and vivid, these artifacts are one piece in the strategy to resuscitate the region. The pictures belong to Monson Arts, which along with the public library keep the old school from going vacant. Later in the year, Monson Arts moves to an elegantly restored building 500 yards or so down the hill on the main street lakeshore. It pairs on a block there with an already complete art gallery and a general store offering a wine selection merchandised for condominium dwellers from southern New England, who may tour here or who may never show up.

These fixtures, with studios and dwellings for visiting artists, are part of a vision for Monson — a rebuild with millions from a private foundation designed to transform the place into an arts colony.

The Portland-based Libra Foundation — a nonprofit with its own idiosyncratic roots — is Monson's white knight. It has $200 million rooted in the fortune of the late Betty Noyce. Its method, built on the vision of Noyce, is "catalytic" giving — using aggressive investment to spur economic growth in Maine.

Noyce retreated to a seaside home in Bremen, Maine, after her 22-year marriage broke up in the mid-1970s. It was no ordinary divorce. She was married to Robert Noyce, a co-inventor of the microchip and a founder of Intel — an engine of the gig economy. When Robert decided to marry an Intel executive in 1975, California divorce laws directed half a fortune to Betty. Even after decades of gargantuan giving, Betty Noyce's estate was valued at between $100 million and $1 billion when she died in 1996. If the Monson investments work, it will be accurate to say that the invention of the microchip, attended with California community property laws, resuscitated a community in the Moosehead Lake region.

Libra is not releasing the specific dollar amount of its investment, but it is a grand plan estimated in the tens of millions. It is rehabilitating more than 30 buildings near the lakefront. Studios, seminars, and juried opportunities for summer artist retreats are all in the offing. The former elementary school will keep the public library and add medical and dental services.

There is plenty of skepticism in the region about whether this flatlander vision can sink roots. Andrew Costello moved to the town of Bradford, Maine 15 years ago after running a Gateway computer store for many years in the Midwest. His Bradford General Store has grown, selling groceries, beer, and snacks — things he says people commuting south to Bangor want. The Monson General Store is 38 miles west, so no threat to his business. Still, he has visited it and, with no rancor, offers his blunt assessment. "There's a lot of stupid money going in there."

The man has a point. Of course, this being a thinned-out frontier, there is hefty commercial risk whether you are buying a skidder or cases of sauvignon blanc. Two home-towners, Tyler Adkins, who ran unsuccessfully for the Legislature, and his younger brother John laugh darkly at the perpetual standoff between the views of commercial traditionalists like Costello and others who are thinking out of the box. The brothers are entrapped between these camps

— those who say things can't or shouldn't be done and those who try, sometimes recklessly and sometimes with potential.

John Adkins moved back after college in North Carolina and work promoting sports enterprises, the National Football League's Carolina Panthers and golf tournaments. One of his three jobs now is helping promote the region. Central to this effort is Greenville, 14 miles north of Monson on the shores of Moosehead Lake — remote, spectacular, and defensive to change.

A wall to change got built there about 15 years ago when a development company affiliated with paper company landowners proposed a resort near Moosehead Lake with more than 900 house lots and two recreational vehicle parks. Locals and the statewide Natural Resources Council beat the stuffing out the idea. It never happened and likely was never economically viable anyway. A 2019 assessment of whether a 60-room hotel with some meeting space in Greenville would have enough business to survive showed the concept barely feasible.

The risk to Greenville these days is that they could be left with arguably the most spectacular lake east of the Mississippi River and no viable community to go with it. Enrollment at the consolidated middle and high school is down from 359 in 1999 to about 200 now. The hospital is vulnerable to closure. In a lake region about the size of Delaware, and with only 4,000 residents, the pragmatic necessity for economic developers here is to get 200 more year-round residents.

Local people are coming around to the idea that making Greenville more welcoming to visitors and potential newcomers is not a threat. Hordes are not coming and, if they did, they would find more than 60 percent of this massive region already locked down, in publicly owned lands or permanent conservation easements. This paradise is not changeable — unless the potential loss of schools, Laker high school basketball, the post office, the hospital, and people, count as change.

John Adkins is not involved in the Libra effort in Monson — other than as a part-time waiter at The Quarry, a Monson restaurant opened with Libra support. In regional reactions to the gussied town just a state highway hop from

Greenville's giant emerald of a lake, he hears the voices of people down for too long.

"It is not necessarily wanting it to fail, but just waiting for it to fail so they can say, 'Yeah, I knew it wouldn't work' versus looking at it and saying, 'This is great because it's the gateway to our region and we can build on that.' "

No matter, the Adkins boys are hanging in. Unfazed by losing one election, Tyler Adkins runs for the Monson Board of Selectmen four months later and wins. He continues to work for UGE remotely, remodels his house and barn, and sees broadband access chugging ahead from just one road to most of the town. One of his first successes on the board is unsticking resistance to a change that towns all over the Northeast are jumping on — buying back streetlights from utilities and installing LED lights. Monson will save $5,500 per year in fixed cost through the change.

Tyler's method now is pulling opportunity into his paradise two hours north of Portland. He is installing a solar array on one of his 34 acres, enough to power 24 homes. Homeowners and local businesses already have fully subscribed his grid.

"I really believe that a drone-video Facebook ad of this place might be sufficient to get certain people to move to Monson from New York City," he says. "They don't want to live in stupid, suburban New Jersey."

The number of optimists in town is edging along. John Wentworth, the former owner of furniture-maker Moosehead Manufacturing, saw the Libra initiative clearly from the start. "Our town won the lottery," he says with a chuckle.

The investment, as he sees it, is substantial, serious, and coming to a place with a soul for making stuff work.

Wentworth remembers details — like the fact that Moosehead Manufacturing's run in Monson never would have existed without serendipitous goodwill. His business had a predecessor called Monson Wood Crafters. That outfit started in 1945 with investments from town fathers concerned that veterans coming back from World War II would have no place to work.

Within a couple of years, Monson Wood Crafters went bankrupt. Wentworth's great uncle, Tolford Durham, was traveling the state in those days as what he called a wood cruiser — a woodsman who matched sources of specific lumber to commercial customers. Tolford saw the downed Monson operation as something his brother, Wentworth's grandfather John Durham, could help turn around. He was right. John Durham had a Harvard MBA and had become expert in manufacturing processes working for the Diamond Match Company.

The brothers put the Wood Crafters shop back online. During the next few years, the Durham brothers did something else that was not required. All those small-town businesspeople — shopkeepers and insurance agents — who put up investments in the old company that failed got made whole by the new company. The 60-year run of Moosehead Manufacturing, with peak employment of 250 people, began with an old-school commercial ethos stubbornly alive in the rural Second. The circle completed in 2007, when consumer taste for disposable furniture and supply chains fitted to an Ikea market pushed Moosehead Manufacturing out of business and John Wentworth shielded suppliers and employees from the worst.

Wentworth could have left Monson then. He had job offers in North Carolina, a more robust furniture region also getting squeezed. He stayed put. He bought a drafty old potato barn on the road to Dover and began making furniture there himself. His wife, Melinda, says now, pointing to the holes in John's sneakers, that he is "a rugged, frugal New Englander."

The fact that at least Monson will be saved through millions invested via Libra is believable because clear-eyed characters like Wentworth believe it. He sees the picture, assessing that the quality of rural life that kept him and Melinda in Monson for decades is precisely what Libra is leveraging.

"They've made some good decisions, by doing it right and not doing it half-assed," John says. "These buildings they are building down here are better built than when they were built here originally, by far." And, he adds, Libra knows "it's about economic development," inclusive of agriculture and tourism at minimum, and not the concept of an arts colony alone.

National politics bounced through these counties without getting too close to the communal life and death struggles of places like Monson, Atkinson, Greenville, and dozens of others. The rules are different in that game. In paradise, where the sun rises first, most citizens play with one rule, one understanding: People need a little space to look for their smooth stones and no one should be foolish enough to dim the light on earth's last, best hope.

NOTES

Chapter 1

Depending on exact location and seasons, other Maine places in the Second can claim to see the sunrise first. Eastport and, from March to September, Mars Hill are other major contenders in the first sunrise space.

Sunrise-watching crowd on Cadillac. More detail on the crowd and their interests: New England Travel Today, Sunrise on Cadillac Mountain, July 3, 2018 at https://newengland.com/today/travel/maine/sunrise-cadillac-mountain/

National Park Service, Written in Acadia's Rocks, last updated March 16, 2015 at https://www.nps.gov/articles/written-in-acadias-rocks.htm

Portland Press Herald, "Nation's eyes on Maine's 2nd District," Steve Collins, Oct. 7, 2018 at https://www.pressherald.com/2018/10/07/maines-2nd-district-race-among-the-liveliest-in-the-nation/

Boston Globe, "Democrats target New England's GOP House holdout," Liz Goodwin, Feb. 10, 2018.

Chapter 2

The percentages of donors from different geographic areas are calculated from the following Federal Election Commission reports: Committee to Elect Jared Golden, 2018, Financial Summary, accessed October 2018, and Poliquin for Congress, 2018, Financial Summary, accessed October 2018.

Portland Press Herald, "Most per vote, $131, spent on Golden in 2nd District," Noel K. Gallagher, Nov. 18, 2018.

"Do Members of Congress Ever Lose Re-Election," Tom Murse, ThoughtCo, Jan. 24, 2018 at https://www.thoughtco.com/do-congressmen-ever-lose-re-election-3367511

Chapter 3

Associated Press, "Maine governor: Asylum seekers bring disease like 'ziki fly,' February 17, 2016.

The Spectator, "Trump before Trump," Adam Robinson, March 17, 2016 at http://the-spectator.com/2016/03/18/trump-before-trump/

Chapter 4
Piscataquis Observer, "The Plight of Small Town Maine," Andy Torbett, April 12, 2018 at https://observer-me.com/2018/04/12/the-plight-of-small-town-maine/

Chapter 5

No notes

Chapter 6

The Maine Woods: A Fully Annotated Edition, Henry David Thoreau, edited by Jeffrey S. Cramer, Yale University Press, New Haven and London, 2009.

Chapter 7

Diary of Frederic Talbot, East Machias, Maine, transcribed by Barbara T. Whittier, August, 1946, University of Maine, Special Collections, Orono, Maine.

Pope and Talbot Inc., International Directory of Company Histories, Thomas Gale, 2006 at https://www.encyclopedia.com/books/politics-and-business-magazines/pope-and-talbot-inc

Historical Atlas of Maine, Stephen J. Hornsby, Richard W. Judd, and Michael J. Hermann, University of Maine Press, Orono, Maine, 2015.

The Yankee Exodus, Stewart H. Holbrook, University of Washington Press, Seattle, 1950, p. 253.

Chapter 8

Stand Firm Ye Boys From Maine, Thomas A. Desjardin, Thomas Publications, Gettysburg, Penn., 1995.

Historical Atlas of Maine, Stephen J. Hornsby, Richard W. Judd, and Michael J. Hermann, University of Maine Press, Orono, Maine, 2015.

Joshua Lawrence Chamberlain: A Life in Letters, Thomas Desjardin, The National Civil War Museum, Bloomsbury Publishing, London, 2013.

Note on Civil War casualties: More current demographic studies estimate that Civil War deaths are larger than originally reported. The early and most relied on source was done by Civil War veterans and historians William F. Fox and Frederick H. Dyer.

Their table, "Summary of Losses During the War of the Rebellion," is at http://www.thomaslegion.net/totalcivilwarkilleddeadsoldiers.html.

The telling figures for Maine are the proportion of its losses. Maine had more losses than any New England state except Massachusetts, which had double Maine's population at the time. It is important for context to remember that as a burgeoning natural resources frontier then, Maine had a larger population than Connecticut and New Hampshire in the 1860s; its population also was larger than Rhode Island and Vermont, which it still is now. Looking at proportions, Maine lost substantially. Maine had two-thirds losses of Massachusetts, at half Massachusetts' population size; Maine was 3.6 times bigger in population than Rhode Island and had 7.1 times more losses.

Chapter 9

Washington Post, "Kennedy, Muskie, Jackson Eyed for Nixon Dirty Tricks in '71," George Lardner, Jr. and Walter Pincus, Oct. 30, 1997, page A18.

State of Maine, State Election, September 13, 1954, Maine State Library file accessed October 2018.

Muskie, Lippman, Theo, Jr. and Hansen, Donald C., W.W. Norton and Co., New York, N.Y. ,1971, p. 57 on state party registrations.

Chapter 10
"The Paper Plantation: Ralph Nader's study group report on the pulp and paper industry in Maine," William C. Osborn, Grossman Publishers, New York, N.Y., 1974.

The so-called "Powell memo" quoted at the beginning of Chapter 10 was written in August 1971 by Lewis Powell, Jr., then a lawyer, to a neighbor and friend active with the U.S. Chamber of Commerce. The memo describes a storm rolling into free enterprise – consisting not just of "Communists" and "revolutionaries" but "perfectly respectable elements of society: from the college campus, the pulpit, the media, the intellectual and literary journals, the arts and sciences, and from politicians." A few months later, President Nixon nominated Powell to the U.S. Supreme Court. Activists like to point to the Powell memo as some sort of architectural drawing for everything from libertarian think tanks to Bill O'Reilly. Reading its dusty prose and repackaged quotes from the Wall Street Journal and Fortune it is hard to see it generating much more than an invoice. It is an artifact – one of thousands (including of the Paper Plantation report) – that point to the early 1970s as a stupefying time for commercial players accustomed to holding most of the cards. Nader matters more because he is the change agent, drawing fire and becoming the archetype for a fight that will divide people more neatly and consistently into camps.
The full memo: Powell, Lewis F. Jr. (August 23, 1971), "Attack of American Free Enterprise System" can be found at --
https://www.thirteen.org/wnet/supremecourt/personality/sources_document13.html

Chapter 11
Portland Press Herald, "Maine has more at stake on health care than most other states," Charles Lawton, Oct. 3, 2017.

The New Yorker, "How Medicare Was Made," Julian E. Zelizer, Feb. 15, 2015.

Figures on U.S. health care spending over time from Peterson-Kaiser Health System Tracker at https://www.healthsystemtracker.org/chart-collection/u-s-spending-healthcare-changed-time/#item-start

Chapter 12
On Writing, King, Stephen, Scribner, New York, N.Y., 2000, p.59

(Income by Congressional District) U.S. Census Bureau, American Community Survey at https://www.census.gov/mycd/?st=23&cd=02, retrieved March 12, 2019.

County Health Rankings and Roadmaps, Robert Wood Johnson Foundation at –
https://www.rwjf.org/en/how-we-work/grants-explorer/featured-programs/county-health-ranking-roadmap.html

Chapter 13
New York Times, "Political Cameos on 'The Good Wife'? Donna Brazile Likes Them," Mike Hale, Oct. 1, 2014.

There are many earlier episodes and battles around preservation and uses of Maine forests. Author Phyllis Austin documents the depth of the conflicts Quimby entered in her outstanding book, Queen Bee. Queen Bee, Phyllis Austin, Tilbury House Publishers, Thomaston, Maine, 2015.

The New Yorker, "Honey Dance," Tad Friend, July 20, 2014 at https://www.newyorker.com/magazine/2014/07/28/honey-dance

Forbes, "Maine vs Thoreau: The Roxanne Quimby Question," Michael Charles Tobias, Oct. 3, 2011.

Roll Call, "Democrats eying Maine natives to unseat Bruce Poliquin," Simone Pathe', July 20, 2017

Portland Press Herald, "Lucas St. Clair should step out of the dark money shadows," Bill Nemitz, May 10, 2018.

Lewiston Sun Journal, "Congressional contender Tim Rich alleges 'rigged game' in Democratic primary," Steve Collins, Feb. 8, 2018.

Note on Golden being underestimated: Golden had the opportunity to run in a legislative district considered safe for Democrats. The Democrat who preceded Golden got 60 percent of the vote in 2012; Golden got 62 percent in 2014. Before the congressional race, he had not faced a race he could lose so the idea that he was untested gave hope to primary opponents.

Chapter 14

Lewiston Sun Journal, "Jared Golden: From combat to candidate for Congress," Steve Collins, Sept. 9, 2018,
https://www.sunjournal.com/2018/09/09/jared-golden-from-combat-to-candidate-for-congress/

Lewiston Sun Journal, "Bruce Poliquin: Ignoring the 'noise' to help others," Steve Collins, Sept. 23, 2018
https://www.sunjournal.com/2018/09/22/bruce-poliquin-ignoring-the-noise-to-help-others/

Chapter 15

Lewiston Sun Journal, "Bruce Poliquin's Wall Street past raises questions," Steve Collins, Nov. 2, 2016
https://www.sunjournal.com/2016/11/02/bruce-poliquins-wall-street-past-raises-questions/

Lewiston Sun Journal, "Despite ruffling feathers, Poliquin vows to remain 'activist treasurer,' "Steve Mistler, Sept. 18, 2011.

Associated Press, "Poliquin goes on attack against GOP rival Otten," David Sharp, Mary 10, 2010.

Associated Press, "Rep. Bruce Poliquin to give away Wells Fargo campaign donation," Oct. 5, 2016 at https://www.sunjournal.com/2016/10/05/rep-bruce-poliquin-give-away-wells-fargo-campaign-donation/

Poliquin's early bids were a marker that the established Republican operatives in Maine, more comfortable with candidates like Sen. Olympia Snowe, were seeing more aggressive messages and tactics take hold. They underestimated the appeal of Gov. LePage's rhetoric and the perseverance of newcomers like Poliquin.

Chapter 16
Lewiston Sun Journal, "War veteran attending Bates still has heart in Afghanistan," Bonnie Washuk, Nov. 9, 2009.

BBC News, "Timeline: Iraq War," July 5, 2016.

Associated Press, "A timeline of U.S. troop levels in Afghanistan since 2001," July 6, 2016 at https://www.militarytimes.com/news/your-military/2016/07/06/a-timeline-of-u-s-troop-levels-in-afghanistan-since-2001/

CTC Sentinel, Afghanistan's Heart of Darkness, Brian Glyn Williams, November 2008, Vol. 1, Issue 12, at https://ctc.usma.edu/afghanistans-heart-of-darkness-fighting-the-taliban-in-kunar-province/

Operation Steel Curtain Concludes Along Iraq-Syria Border, American Forces Press Release, Nov. 22, 2005.

Washington Post Foreign Service, "U.S. Airstrikes take toll on civilians," Dec. 24, 2005.

Lewiston Sun Journal, "Jared Golden: From combat to candidate for Congress," Steve Collins, Sept. 9, 2018.

Chapter 17
News Bates College, "Folks Back Home," Doug Hubley, April 21, 2010 at https://www.bates.edu/news/2010/04/21/folks-back-home/

Federal Election Commission reports: Cain for Congress, 2014, Financial Summary, accessed October 2018; Cain for Congress, 2016, Financial Summary, accessed October 2018, Poliquin for Congress, 2014, Financial Summary, accessed October 2018, Poliquin for Congress, 2016, Financial Summary, accessed October 2018.

Bangor Daily News, "The man behind Maine's GOP upstarts: Political strategist Brent Littlefield engineered LePage, Poliquin victories," Mario Moretto, Jan. 5, 2015 at https://bangordailynews.com/2015/01/04/the-point/the-man-behind-maines-gop-upstarts-political-strategist-brent-littlefield-engineered-lepage-poliquin-victories/

Chapter 18
Lewiston Sun Journal, "New attack ad in heated 2nd District race takes Jared Golden to task for his tattoos," Steve Collins, August 27, 2018.

News Bates College, "Folks Back Home," Doug Hubley, April 21, 2010 at https://www.bates.edu/news/2010/04/21/folks-back-home/

Chapter 19
A Divided and Pessimistic Electorate, Pew Research Center, Nov. 10, 2016 at http://www.people-press.org/2016/11/10/a-divided-and-pessimistic-electorate/

Washington Post, "It's time to bust the myth: Most Trump voters were not working class," June 5, 2017.

Boston Globe, "Mainers defend Somali neighbors against Trump," August 6, 2016 at https://www.bostonglobe.com/metro/2016/08/05/maine-sees-somalian-community-starkly-different-than-what-donald-trump-portrayed/qOh4IjKY3VYYcxNG7zkcBM/story.html

Chapter 20
Census of Population and Housing, at Census.gov.

Furniture Today, Jeff Linville, Feb. 21, 2007.

Chapter 21
Office of Family Assistance, U.S. Department of Health and Human Services, TANF Caseload Data 2018 and AFDC Caseload Data, 1960 to 1995 at https://www.acf.hhs.gov/ofa/programs/tanf/data-reports

Chapter 22
The New York Times, "The Five Battlegrounds for Control of the U.S. House, Profile: Maine's Second District," Jonathan Martin, Sept. 19, 2018.

Portland Press Herald, "Gun owners speak out," Megan Gray, March 19,2018 at https://www.pressherald.com/2018/03/18/we-are-gun-owners/

Portland Press Herald, "On gun laws, Jared Golden thinks just like most Mainers," Bill Nemitz, Sept. 13, 2018.

Chapter 23 to Chapter 26
No notes

Chapter 27
Letters of Note, "Wind the clock, for tomorrow is another day," January 6, 2012 at http://www.lettersofnote.com/2012/01/wind-clock-for-tomorrow-is-another-day.html

Chapter 28

U.S. District Court, District of Maine, Brett Baber, et al., v. Matthew Dunlap, et al., No. 1:18-CV-465-LEW.

Chapter 29

Photographers on Photography: A Critical Anthology, Nathan Lyons, editor, Prentice-Hall, Englewood, NJ, 1966.

New York Times, "Elizabeth B. Noyce, 65, Benefactor of Maine with Vast Settlement from Her Divorce," Sept. 20, 1996.

ACKNOWLEDGMENTS

My appreciation to readers who kept this story on track: Ken Habarta, Rick Ramseyer, Dianne Turpin, and editing wizard Betsy Gattis.

There are a number of people and organizations not quoted in the text who provided essential insight about the experience of people in the Second District: Patrick Strauch, executive director of the Maine Forest Products Council; Yellow Light Breen, president and CEO of Maine Development Foundation; Steve Levesque and Luke Muzzy of the Moosehead Lake Region Economic Development Corporation; Monson Arts; Jemma Gascoine; Catherine Reilly Delutio, economist and CEO of Rangeley Trading Company; Lubec's own Miles Unobsky Theeman, board member of Maine Maritime Academy and the eastern most person who knows the location of the Volvo line; Kelly MacFadyn and her team at School Administrative District 4, including John Keane, principal at Piscataquis Community High School, Deborah McPhail, assistance principal and guidance director, and Jessica Dunton, assistant principal and district technology director at Piscataquis Community Elementary School, Jerry Caron, Destiny Demo, Thomas Kittredge, Mike Hurley, and Cary Olson.

Vital assistance with research: Desiree Butterfield-Nagy of the Special Collections Department at the University of Maine's Fogler Library; Marcela Peres and staff at the Lewiston Public Library, the Glickman Family Library at the University of Southern Maine; the Maine State Library and the Law and Legislative Reference Library in Augusta; Curtis Memorial Library in Brunswick and Merrill Memorial Library in Yarmouth.

Thanks to all the candidates, and their teams, on the Maine playing field: They do not always play nice, but collectively they do more to interrupt real dangers to democracy than their national peers.

Thanks also to two people who said I should write this thing when it was just a notion: Glenn Picher and David Turin; to the Hartland natives: Charlene Babnaw, Erica Harbarta, Lisa Bergman, and Dick Randlett.

Also, to everyone at Hannaford, and especially Eric Blom, Sherri Stevens, and Bruce Daman, because, like the Second, you are wicked smart.

And special thanks to Ben, Ted, and Tori Norton, who never asked, "Why are you going to Piscataquis County again?"

ABOUT THE AUTHOR

Michael Norton's family roots in Maine date to 1937 when his grandfather bought a near-abandoned sporting camp on Great Moose Lake in Hartland, Maine. A graduate of the University of Minnesota, he has worked as a daily newspaper journalist in both Minnesota and Maine and worked in government as a legislative liaison and in the private sector as a marketing executive. He is a board member of the Harvard Pilgrim Health Care Foundation and the Susan Curtis Foundation. Michael lives in Maine, with his wife, Tori, sons, Ben and Ted, and an excitable dog. He is a flatlander.

Made in the USA
Middletown, DE
30 October 2019